AIR TRAFFIC CONTROL

9TH EDITION

Graham Duke

Ian Allan
PUB···

CONTENTS

Acknowledgements

I am extremely grateful to all those who, once again, co-operated with me in the preparation of this publication. Without their help, and their agreement for me to use many of the illustrations which appear in the book, my task would have been considerably harder.

My thanks also to Enid for her patience and assistance throughout.

Front cover: **Delta Airlines Boeing 767-200.** *Delta Airlines*

Front cover background: **Cleared flight level and vertical assistance window, part of the programme developed as a simulated control experience.** *DM Aviation/Dale McLoughlin*

Title page: **Long-range radar station, Great Dun Fell.** *Author*

First published 2005

ISBN 0 7110 3074 X

Published by Ian Allan Publishing

an imprint of Ian Allan Publishing Ltd, Hersham, Surrey KT12 4RG.
Printed in England by Ian Allan Printing Ltd, Hersham, Surrey KT12 4RG.

Code: 0507/C2

Visit the Ian Allan Publishing website at
www.ianallanpublishing.co.uk

For many airlines, air transport in Europe is certainly a boom industry at present. This is partially due to a return to the period of steady growth experienced before the terrorist attacks of 11 September 2001, but, more significantly, to the rapid expansion of the low-cost carriers.

Even though the increase in the cheaper end of the market is expected to peak within a relatively short time, EUROCONTROL still anticipates that the number of aircraft operating within its airspace will increase by 250% by the year 2025.

The low-cost boom is not without a downside for the air traffic service providers. Many of these flights are being operated from previously under-used airports, which generally do not have the benefit of access to fully controlled airspace. Instead, aircraft must cross through airspace in which other categories of users may be encountered — for example, military jets, light aircraft, gliders, etc.

Although the UK Civil Aviation Authority is very much aware of the situation and keeps each case under constant review, others in the business feel very strongly that these passenger jets are being placed at unnecessary risk. Having to fly in uncontrolled airspace is considered by many to be inappropriate for such flights.

The British Airline Pilots Association, BALPA, concerned about the number of Airprox incidents occurring outside controlled airspace, has advised UK airlines to avoid uncontrolled airspace wherever possible, even though in some cases it can be financially beneficial.

Another issue is the amount of revenue being generated. In general, the low-cost carriers operate only short-haul sectors, and much of their time in UK airspace is spent either climbing or descending, requiring considerably more input from air traffic control (ATC) than, for example, high-level Atlantic traffic.

The income derived by ATC from these flights is, therefore, proportionately much less, compared with overflights, particularly when the North Atlantic traffic has been slow to recover.

Privatising the System

In 2001 public attention was focused on the controversial public/private partnership of the British air traffic services provider, under which the state sold off 51% of the business and retained a 49% interest. ATC employees were offered 5% of the privately funded element.

The successful bid for the private element was submitted by a consortium of leading UK airlines (consisting of British Airways, British Midland, Virgin Atlantic, Airtours, Britannia, JMC, Monarch and easyJet, and known as The Airline Group) for a 46% share of the air traffic control business.

The partnership, involving the UK Government and National Air Traffic Services (NATS), has been strongly criticised for failing to anticipate the possible effects of a sudden drop in income from an unexpected event.

This, of course, is exactly what happened in 2001, leaving NATS in a precarious financial position. Eventually, in 2003, a £65 million investment from the British Airports Authority (BAA) ensured its continued operation, and at the same time, two non-executive directors from BAA were appointed to the Board.

The National Audit Office (NAO) was extremely critical of the new arrangements, pointing to an £800 million benefit to the Government, made at the expense of NATS's bank debt. The Public Accounts Committee agreed, commenting that the new relationship left NATS in a vulnerable position as it resulted in a debt which was double that before the public/private partnership. However, in a further report, in January 2004, the NAO endorsed the 2003 refinancing package.

NATS finally moved into the black during the 12-month period to 31 March 2004, with £1.8 million profit, compared with the £29.1 million loss the previous year and the £79.9 million loss the year before that. Forecasts indicate that this will continue to improve.

EUROCONTROL, in 2002, had placed NATS as the overall second least cost-effective air navigation service provider of a total of 32 European states but positive improvements are expected at all levels.

The New En-Route Centres

Another significant recent event was the opening of the new ATC en-route centre at Swanwick, in Hampshire, on 27 January 2002, taking over most of the en-route control responsibilities from the former RAF station at West Drayton in Middlesex.

British Airways Airbus A320. British Airways

Although a few teething problems resulted in a flurry of media attention, the centre has successfully introduced a series of airspace and operational improvements and is considered by most to be a world leader. In fact, after the first two years of virtually flawless performance, delays have been reduced to a record low.

It is worth noting that when a failure of the National Airspace System in June 2004 resulted in significant delays to traffic, and it was immediately assumed that this was caused by problems at Swanwick, it was, in fact, due to software problems at West Drayton.

At Prestwick, Scotland, work on a new en-route centre restarted in June 2004 after an interruption of two years. It is due to enter service in 2009.

Safety Issues

A number of events in Europe during the last few years have damaged public confidence in a system which is, however, still extremely safe. Two collisions on the ground, at Linate airport, Milan, in 2001 and at Charles de Gaulle airport in Paris in 2000, focused attention on the issue of runway incursions, now considered to be the most dangerous part of a public transport flight.

Even after severe criticism of the Linate air traffic management system following the accident, another similar occurrence almost took place three years later at Milan's Malpensa airport, when the pilot of an MD-87 aborted the take-off run after an Airbus A330 was seen further down the runway.

The most significant, and tragic, ATC-related event in European aviation for a generation was, of course, the 2002 mid-air collision between a Russian passenger plane and a British cargo jet over Überlingen, Germany, whilst under the control of Zürich ATC. This accident was a dreadful blow to aviation safety organisations across the world, demonstrating how total safety is so difficult to achieve, and how easily

London Gatwick Visual Control Room.
National Air Traffic Services Ltd

unconnected events can combine to create tragedy. This particular case is covered in detail later in the book.

Another development, leading directly from such ATC-related accidents and near misses, has been the increasing tendency of the authorities to publicly shame, and even prosecute, individual controllers who were unfortunate enough to have been on duty at the time, even though in almost every case systemic failures throughout the management structure have been found to be part of the cause. Several European countries have adopted this approach, leading to a stifling of the reporting by air traffic control personnel of safety-related issues, for fear of being blamed and made scapegoats. In the long term, of course, this can only result in a deterioration of safety standards, not their improvement.

The naming of the controller who happened to be on duty at the time of the German mid-air collision led to the ultimate tragedy when he was murdered at his home by a grief-stricken relative of one of the children who died in the accident.

In another example, concerning the Milan incident mentioned earlier, the tower controller on duty at the time, and the Airport Director, were each sentenced to eight years in prison for 'negligence and manslaughter', and two others were sent down for six and a half years.

Similar charges have been brought in other parts of the world. For example, in the Netherlands in 2000 the Dutch air navigation organisation prosecuted three controllers following a runway incursion. Controllers in Mexico (2000) and Japan (2001) have also faced criminal charges.

Again in the Netherlands, a controller with a 35-year unblemished career was suspended because he refused to operate a new system which he considered to be unsafe.

Since the Dutch events, reporting of incidents by controllers in the Netherlands dropped by half. The message to controllers seems to be 'admit nothing, report nothing'. At a time when there is a critical shortage of controllers in Europe, new recruits will surely be harder to find.

Maastricht Upper Area Control Centre.
EUROCONTROL

The International Federation of Air Traffic Control Associations (IFATCA) has called for legal protection and immunity from prosecution except in situations where there has been a clear case of negligence, and EUROCONTROL is taking the same line.

One Sky for Europe

The complex airspace of Europe is among the world's busiest, with daily traffic levels frequently reaching 30,000 movements. Fundamental changes to the systems and procedures, as well as in the way the service is governed, are essential if gridlock is to be avoided.

EUROCONTROL'S major initiative in this field is the Single Sky programme, whereby European airspace will move away from being dominated by national boundaries to more efficient Functional Airspace Blocks that are designed to produce the best results in air traffic management terms.

In addition to the EUROCONTROL centre at Maastricht, which has controlled the upper airspace of Belgium, the Netherlands, Luxembourg and northwest Germany since 1963, a new centre in Vienna will soon be controlling the upper airspace of eight central European states.

At an international level, both the International Civil Aviation Organisation (ICAO) and the International Air Transport Association (IATA) believe that air traffic services must ultimately be conducted as a global business in preference to the politically dominated state-by-state system which is currently the case.

The inevitable involvement of technology, in the form of computers, satellites and data transmissions, is changing the entire approach to ATC. In the foreseeable future controllers will become airspace managers, monitoring traffic movements which will have been flight planned in four dimensions well before the aircraft leaves the ground.

Across Europe, integration and upgrading of the numerous facilities are an essential prerequisite of a global air traffic

Boeing 747 of Virgin Atlantic. Virgin Atlantic

management system. EUROCONTROL is the multinational body responsible for implementing this major task, through its European Air Traffic Management Programme (EATMP) as part of its role as regulator for en-route air traffic. The UK is also a member of the European Civil Aviation Committee consisting of 38 states with a common objective — the integration and co-ordination of air traffic systems throughout Europe.

Unfortunately, persuading the various European government bodies to recognise and face up to the challenge of a supra-national air transport system has not been an easy task for EUROCONTROL, even though considerable improvements have been achieved.

In 2002 an important step was taken when the European Commission became a member of EUROCONTROL, enabling aviation regulations to be legally enforced throughout the region. This means that EUROCONTROL now has the legal powers to implement its strategic plans for major harmonisation and rationalisation of the airspace of its member states.

Conclusion

Having given a general background to the European and UK ATC system in this Introduction, the rest of the book expands on various separate aspects. Because the book is written with the non-professional in mind, the systems and procedures are explained as simply as possible but without omitting any of the essentials.

None of this would have been possible without the assistance and patience of many professionals in the world of aviation and air traffic control. Without exception, they have been particularly helpful and encouraging and I am pleased to record my gratitude to them.

The business of air traffic control and aviation is, by its very nature, subject to frequent changes, some minor and some quite fundamental. Over the next 20 years technological advances in computers, data transfer and satellites will undoubtedly have a dramatic effect on how air traffic is handled.

Airband Listening

If you are starting out on the hobby of airband listening, one of your primary considerations will be the purchase of a suitable airband receiver. A companion book has been produced for just this subject, also published by Ian Allan. The book, entitled *abc Airband Radio Guide*, now in its sixth edition, gives detailed information on what to look for when choosing which receiver to buy.

1. Airspace Essentials

This chapter explains how the airspace of the United Kingdom is organised, and includes some basic information about operational procedures.

Flight Information Regions

The airspace of the United Kingdom consists of two Flight Information Regions: London and Scottish. Within each region, the airspace below Flight Level 245 (FL245, approximately 24,500ft) is known as a Flight Information Region (FIR). Airspace at and above FL245 is known as the Upper Flight Information Region (UIR).

The FIR/UIR titles 'London' and 'Scottish' are also used as the radio callsigns. A separate FIR/UIR covers the Republic of Ireland, under the jurisdiction of the Irish Aviation Authority, using the callsign 'Shannon'.

Throughout Europe, however, the point of separation between Upper and Lower airspace is inconsistent. In France, for example, the split occurs at FL195.

As part of its programme of harmonisation, EUROCONTROL has decreed that from 2006 FL195 will be implemented in all its member states, including the UK.

The UK Airspace System

All airspace in the United Kingdom is divided into two main classifications: 'controlled' and 'uncontrolled'.

The term 'controlled airspace' is applied to those parts of the system which are operated under a series of rules and

Qatar Airways flight crew. Qatar Airways

Shanwick Oceanic Control Centre, Prestwick.
Shanwick OCC

regulations. These rules are prescribed by National Air Traffic Services Limited, the Civil Aviation Authority and the international governing body, the International Civil Aviation Organisation.

Pilots, and the aircraft they fly, must conform to the rules regarding qualifications, carriage of equipment, operating procedures, etc, before they can fly in controlled airspace.

There are a number of categories of controlled airspace, which are described in detail later. The rules vary considerably in each type, including some where the flight may not be under positive control; for this reason 'controlled airspace' is sometimes referred to as 'regulated airspace'.

Controlled, or regulated, airspace is designed to protect aircraft in flight, both in the en-route phase, and when departing or approaching airports. However, at small, less-used airfields, the volume of traffic and the types of flight, may not justify the creation of controlled airspace.

In these situations the airspace is described as 'uncontrolled' or 'free' airspace. Very few air traffic control rules apply in these cases. Outside controlled airspace pilots may fly where they wish, without mandatory control, provided they comply with a series of common sense rules designed to afford an appropriate level of protection without being unduly restrictive.

Sectors

The UK is divided into a variety of regions, some very large, others quite small, known as sectors. The en-route airways, and the upper air routes within each sector, are the responsibility of a team of controllers operating from the appropriate control centre. Each sector normally has an allocation of one main radio frequency and one or two reserve frequencies. As the traffic proceeds through the airspace, responsibility for each flight passes from one sector team to the next, changing radio frequencies when instructed by the controller.

Details of each flight are presented to the controllers through a system of flight progress strips, which may be in paper format, mounted on plastic holders, or electronically on the radar screen. Each strip is automatically generated approximately 15 minutes before the flight enters the sector.

Classes of Airspace

In 1991 European airspace was redefined into seven different international categories, identified by the letters A, B, C, D, E, F and G. There is no class C airspace in the UK, but this is expected to change in the near future.

Classes A, B, C, D, E and F are controlled (or regulated) airspace, where controllers have certain duties and responsibilities and where the airspace is subject to a number of rules.

Class G airspace is uncontrolled (or free) airspace, where there are no ATC rules, although there are numerous 'Rules of the Air'.

Pilots may fly by using the instruments on the aircraft, known as 'Instrument Flight Rules' (IFR), or by determining the track of the aircraft visually, known as 'Visual Flight Rules' (VFR).

Controllers never refer to the airspace classification system. Instead, their messages will only mention 'controlled' or 'uncontrolled' airspace.

Aerodrome Traffic Zones (which are usually a 1.5-nautical-mile-radius circle around the airfield extending from the surface to a height of 2000ft) have the same status as the surrounding airspace.

Class A Airspace

Class A airspace provides the highest level of protection for aircraft.

In Class A, controllers have responsibility for ensuring that safe separation between all aircraft is maintained at all times. This means that:

■ All flights must be flown under IFR;
■ Flight plans are required;
■ ATC instructions must be followed;
■ Radios must be monitored at all times;
■ Transponders must be operating in height readout mode;
■ Aircraft with 19 or more seats must be operating TCAS (Traffic Alert and Collision Avoidance System) equipment.

In certain circumstances, VFR flights are permitted to enter Class A airspace. This is usually under 'Special VFR' conditions.

Class A airspace applies to:
■ All airways;
■ The Channel Islands Control Area;
■ The London Terminal Manoeuvring Area;
■ The Manchester Terminal Manoeuvring Area;
■ The Shanwick Oceanic Control Area.

The airways system consists of corridors of protected airspace which enable public transport aircraft to route across the country with the benefit of a continuous

Dragonair Cargo Boeing 747-300. Author

control service, usually aided by radar, in which ground controllers assume responsibility for the safe separation of the various flights within the region. The routes are defined by radio navigation beacons dotted around the country. Controllers issue instructions by radio telephone to the pilots of aircraft within the airways and those instructions must be followed.

Airways are at least 10 nautical miles in width, with an upper level of FL245. However, the base levels of airways can vary considerably, from FL50 (5,000ft) to FL150 (15,000ft). Each airway is designed to accommodate the needs of the traffic that will use it, which is why the base levels are so varied.

Outside the airway, the airspace is uncontrolled, and aircraft are not normally permitted to stray beyond the limits of the airway.

More detail on airways can be found in the chapter covering 'Aeronautical Information'.

Class B Airspace

Class B airspace covers all airspace above FL245 (known as upper airspace), in the areas managed by London Control and Scottish Control.

In upper airspace there are no airways, only straight-line routes between navigation points, which are often not supported by radio facilities on the ground. Controllers may allow aircraft to fly outside these routes while remaining in fully controlled airspace at all times.

Essentially, the rules are the same as for Class A airspace, except that, in theory, flights under VFR are permitted. However, in airspace which is authorised for reduced vertical separation (as in the UK) international rules do not permit VFR flights.

Class C Airspace

Class C airspace is very similar to Class B, except that rules concerning VFR flights are slightly less stringent. At present, no UK airspace is currently designated Class

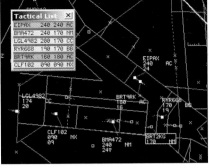

A typical situation display of part of the London Control area.
DM Aviation/Dale McLoughlin

C. However, the upper airspace across most of Europe is already Class C, and the UK is expected to fall into line within a couple of years, as part of the EUROCONTROL strategy for harmonization.

Class D Airspace

Class D airspace covers most airport control area and control zones, with the exception of those in the London and Manchester TMAs (terminal control areas) which are Class A.

Both IFR and VFR flights are allowed, although VFR flights may be refused permission to enter the airspace if the controllers are too busy.

In Class D airspace, ATC will provide separation between all IFR flights. IFR flights will also be given traffic information about VFR flights, but not separation.

VFR flights will be given information about IFR flights and other VFR flights, but they will not be separated from other traffic.

Separation between IFR and VFR flights, and between VFR flights, is the responsibility of the pilots, under the principle of 'see and avoid'.

The rules in Class D airspace are:

- Flight plans are required (but may be given over the radio);
- ATC clearance is required;
- Radio monitoring is required;
- ATC instructions are mandatory.

Pilots must remain outside the airspace until ATC gives permission to enter.

Class E Airspace

Class E airspace covers the Belfast TMA, the Teesside control zone and part of the Scottish TMA. The rules are similar to those in Class D, except that traffic information is given only to VFR pilots who request it. Traffic information will be given to IFR pilots concerning VFR flights which are known to the controller. VFR pilots do not have to obtain a clearance from ATC, or contact it by radio, although they are encouraged to do so.

Class F Airspace

In Class F airspace, controllers will provide advice on separation between those IFR flights which are known to the controller.

Certain routes used by civil flights do not carry the volume of traffic sufficient to justify the status of an airway; these are referred to as 'advisory routes'. Class F airspace covers all advisory routes in the UK.

On these routes the controller will provide an advisory service (not full control) to those aircraft participating in the service to ensure that the rules of separation are applied. The service is available to flights below FL245 but may be limited at low levels due to the inadequate cover of the radar. In such cases it may be possible for pilots to receive a service from a military airfield in the vicinity.

Advisory routes are designated on low-level charts with a letter 'D' — eg W911D is Advisory Route 'Whiskey Nine One One Delta'.

The rules (applicable to participating flights) are:

- Flight plans are required (but may be given over the radio);
- ATC clearance is required;
- Radio communication is required;
- ATC instructions are mandatory.

Class G Airspace

Class G airspace applies to all airspace not included in any of the other classes.

There are no ATC rules concerning flight plans, radios or clearances. However, pilots who are in contact with ATC are expected to follow its instructions. Pilots must also comply with the various rules concerning the use of transponders (above FL100) and the quadrantal flight levels, which are explained in the next chapter.

In Class G airspace, large areas of the UK are covered by the lower airspace radar service (LARS) which is provided by certain civil and military airfields. Although this service is not mandatory, most pilots contact LARS when on cross-country flights.

The Flight Information Service (FIS) is a non-radar service operated from the London and Scottish centres, providing basic information on flights known to the controller.

Pilots flying in Class G airspace (often referred to as 'free' airspace) may request assistance from an Air Traffic Service Unit (ATSU) if they so desire. There are various grades of service, falling within two types: Radar or Non-Radar. These will be covered later.

Control Centres

The UK has several separate airspace regions, each having one or more air traffic control centres, as follows:

London Area Control Centre (LACC)

- Callsign 'London'.
- Based at Swanwick, near Fareham, Hampshire.
- Responsible for en-route traffic throughout most of England and Wales and the surrounding sea areas.
  This centre commenced operations on 27 January 2001, taking over responsibility for en-route traffic in London airspace, which had

previously been managed from West Drayton.

London Terminal Control Centre (LTCC)
- Callsign 'London'.
- Based at RAF West Drayton, Middlesex.
- Responsible for traffic in the London Terminal Area, covering the lower airspace over Greater London.
  It is planned to move LTCC to Swanwick within a few years.

Manchester Area Control Centre (MACC)
- Callsign 'Manchester'.
- Based at Manchester airport.
- Responsible for traffic in the north of England up to and including Flight Level 275.
  It is planned to close Manchester and transfer its operations to the new Scottish Centre after it opens in 2009.

Shannon Area Control Centre.
EUROCONTROL

Scottish Air Traffic Control Centre (SCATCC)
- Callsign 'Scottish'.
- Based near Prestwick airport.
- Responsible for traffic over Scotland, Northern Ireland and part of the North Sea. (The area covered by Scottish is the largest in Europe.)
  This centre is being replaced by new facilities which are in the course of construction.

Oceanic Control Centre (OACC)
- Callsign 'Shanwick'.
- Based near Prestwick airport.
- Responsible for flights over the eastern half of the north Atlantic.

Shannon Air Traffic Control Centre, Shannon
- Callsign 'Shannon'.
- Based near Shannon airport.
- Responsible for traffic in the Republic of Ireland.
  This centre is the responsibility of the Irish Aviation Authority.

Sectorisation

Controllers at the main ATC centres manage the traffic under their jurisdiction through a system of regions, known as 'sectors'. Traffic within each sector is the responsibility of a team of controllers, usually employing one radio frequency for controller/pilot communication.

Each sector is designed to give the most efficient management of the traffic flows; therefore they vary considerably in extent, according to the number of flights that can normally be expected and their phases of flight. For example, a sector which normally handles only high-flying en-route traffic will usually be much larger than (say) a busy sector dealing with a large volume of climbing and descending traffic. In each case, daily predictions of traffic flows determine the capacity for each sector.

Where the maximum volume could be exceeded, the traffic planners may decide to re-route some of the flights through a quieter sector, implement flow restrictions to temporarily limit the number of flights or subdivide the sector into two, with an additional team of controllers to deal with the extra load.

Alternatively, during quiet periods, two or even three sectors will be combined into one, using a single radio frequency for the whole area.

In some parts of the UK sectors are split vertically, so that one team of controllers will handle traffic at lower levels, while its colleagues will manage the flights at high level, each team being on different radio frequencies.

As each flight approaches the edge of a particular sector, the pilot will be instructed to change to the radio frequency allocated to the next sector. It is a fundamental principle that the handover of a flight is co-ordinated with the next sector, although this is often achieved through a range of 'standing agreements' between the sectors.

For example, one such agreement may specify that every flight bound for Heathrow, and approaching from the west on Airway Lima 9, will cross a specified navigation point at a particular flight level. Only in cases where this restriction cannot be achieved will the next sector be advised, and acceptance of the flight co-ordinated.

Most of the sectors operate within the standing agreement system.

Crossair Saab 2000. *Author*

Terminal Manoeuvring Areas (TMAs)

These are blocks of airspace designed to protect groups of adjacent aerodromes and major intersections of airways. In the UK region there are terminal areas at London, Manchester, Belfast and in Scotland, with the Scottish Terminal Area containing airports at Prestwick, Glasgow and Edinburgh.

TMA boundaries are often irregular in shape, with lower levels which vary at different points according to traffic requirements. The London TMA has a number of sub-divisions with differing lower levels, most of which are around 5,000ft. The upper level is 24,500ft for the whole area. The levels are arranged to coincide with the various airways which connect with the terminal area. The London TMA has undergone significant structural changes during the last few years as part of the strategy for improved capacity in UK airspace.

Types of Control Service
Radar Control

This involves the provision of a control service to aircraft using information derived from radar. It is mandatory for

London Area Control Centre, Swanwick, Hampshire. Author

flights using the airways, the upper airspace or the Class A terminal airspace. Most civil passenger and freight-carrying aircraft in UK airspace route under the surveillance of area radar control. Military traffic using the airways or upper air routes also comes within the jurisdiction of the civil air traffic control system.

Upper Air Routes

Above FL245, in the Upper Airspace Control Area (Class B airspace), airways are replaced by Upper Air Traffic Service Routes, with no defined width. Although often referred to as airways, Upper ATS routes are simply straight lines between radio navigation beacons or geographical positions, known as Name Code Designators.

These are points, defined by their respective latitudes and longitudes, which have no supporting facilities on the ground. They all have five letters, and are always quoted in upper case letters. Some have names which relate to a local landmark or town, but many are selected at random. They normally indicate positions where routes intersect, at changes in base levels of airways (in lower airspace) or on international boundaries.

Because aircraft above FL245 are under control, the controllers will usually be prepared to allow pilots to route directly between distant positions which takes the flight many miles away from the routes as shown on the charts. The implementation of long-range area navigation, based on the use of on-board navigation equipment, enables flights to follow precise routes without reference to ground-based facilities.

Radar Services Outside Controlled Airspace

When flying outside controlled airspace, pilots may still be able to take advantage of an ATC service backed up by radar. These can be in the form of 'advice' or 'information'.

■ Radar Advisory Service (RAS)

This is a service where the pilot is given advice on avoiding other flights. The pilot is expected to follow that advice. A Radar Advisory Service will only be offered to flights operating under Instrument Flight Rules.

If the pilot decides not to take the advice of the controller, he must inform ATC, and change the service to a Radar Information Service (see below). The pilot then becomes responsible for any further avoiding action.

The controller will specify the type of service he or she is providing, and this must be read back by the pilot. If the controller's workload is high, or if the radar contact is poor, he or she may be unable to provide an advisory service, in which case the pilot must accept an information service.

■ Radar Information Service (RIS)

Under this service pilots will be given details of the positions, distances and levels (if known) of other aircraft to enable them to decide on any avoiding action which may be appropriate. A Radar Information Service may be provided when it is not possible or practical to provide a Radar Advisory Service.

RAS and RIS may be provided by air traffic control centres, military airfields or civilian airfields, as appropriate. Pilots operating at low level usually transfer from one radar unit to the next as they route across country, provided, of course, the radar units are operating and are within range. The controller will always inform the pilot of the type of service being provided.

Commercial flights operating from an airport that does not have the benefit of controlled airspace connecting it to the

A typical ATC transmitter mast. Author

airways system will normally be given a Radar Advisory Service.

■ **Lower Airspace Radar Service (LARS)**

This is a discretionary service provided by radar controllers at civil and military aerodromes to aircraft in uncontrolled airspace within 30 nautical miles of the aerodrome, usually flying at between 3,000ft and FL95.

The service is advisory and not mandatory; therefore there may be aircraft in the area of which the controller may not be aware. The service is limited to the hours of operation of each participating unit, which may not be open at certain periods. There may also be limited service when aircraft are near the limit of radar cover. Aircraft will be given advice on conflicting traffic in the area. Also, aircraft must be flown in accordance with the quadrantal rule (described later).

■ **Middle Airspace Radar Advisory Service**

Aircraft flying in middle uncontrolled airspace between FL100 and FL245 may contact the Middle Airspace Radar Advisory Service at one of eight military control centres when within range. Aircraft may receive an advisory service to ensure adequate separation between aircraft at the same flight level that are known to the controller. However, as the service is not mandatory other aircraft may be operating in the area without the knowledge of the controller. Also the service may be limited when aircraft are flying near the edge of radar coverage, or when the controller is particularly busy with other traffic.

Non-Radar (Procedural) Service

When a radar service is not available, pilots can request a 'procedural' (ie non-radar) information service, in which pilots are provided with standard separation details based on the information given by pilots on positions and levels.

There is no legal requirement for pilots to request the services of an air traffic unit when outside controlled airspace. For this reason it is possible that some aircraft will not be in contact with any controllers. ATSUs can only offer advice or information to the pilots of aircraft that participate in the available service.

Flight Information Service

Any aircraft in Class G airspace may use the country-wide Flight Information Service which is available on one of several frequencies. Pilots are not obliged to contact the service but it is available for advice and information. It is not the same as being under control. Flights generally route from one aerodrome area to the next, taking advantage of the Flight Information Service in the uncontrolled airspace between aerodrome radar areas. The FIS offers information concerning weather, conflicting traffic, airport conditions, liaison between aerodrome control areas and clearances to join or cross airways. Since airways and TMAs have a lower level, aircraft may pass beneath them and remain in uncontrolled airspace. Aircraft in uncontrolled airspace have to comply with certain rules. Basically they must fly on a 'see and be seen' rule, or, if weather conditions are unsuitable, on instrument flying rules. They are known respectively as Visual Flight Rules and Instrument Flight Rules, abbreviated to VFR and IFR.

Flight Conditions and Flight Rules

Flight conditions relate to the prevailing weather, defining minimum flight visibility and distances from cloud. There are two types of flight conditions:

■ Visual meteorological conditions (VMC) or 'Victor Mike';

■ Instrument meteorological conditions (IMC) or 'India Mike'.

Visual meteorological conditions specify minimum distances from cloud, both horizontally and vertically, and different flight visibilities which are applied according to the circumstances.

These depend upon:
- The class of airspace;
- The speed of the aircraft;
- The level of the aircraft;
- The type of aircraft;
- Whether passengers are being carried.

In the case of low-level flights (at or below 3,000ft), the pilot must always be clear of cloud and in sight of the surface, with a flight visibility of 5km or 1,500 metres (depending on aircraft speed).

Instrument meteorological conditions apply where VMC cannot be complied with.

A pilot who intends to fly in controlled airspace in IMC must have an instrument rating.

A pilot who intends to fly in an airway, or in any other Class A airspace, or above FL245, must have an instrument rating regardless of the weather conditions.

However, pilots do not have to be qualified to fly on instruments to be able to fly under Instrument Flight Rules when outside controlled airspace.

There are also two types of Flight Rules. These define the rules that apply to pilots according to the conditions of their licences:
- Visual Flight Rules (VFR)
- Instrument Flight Rules (IFR)

Pilots who are not qualified to fly on instruments, or who intend flying an aircraft which is not certified for instrument flight, may only do so if they can remain at all times within the appropriate minimum weather conditions. These are referred to as VFR flights.

It is the pilot's responsibility to comply with the privileges of his licence, including pre-planning the flight based on current weather forecasts and in accordance with the rules of the air.

Air traffic controllers will not give an opinion on the suitability of the flight conditions.

Visual Flight Rules mean that an aircraft must be flown according to the conditions that apply to the particular flight. In other words, the rules require an aircraft to be flown in conditions that are equal to, or better than, the specified visual meteorological conditions.

Also, if the flight is to take place in controlled airspace, the pilot must:
- File a flight plan;
- Keep a listening watch on the radio;
- Comply with ATC instructions.

Instrument Flight Rules are also quite simple:
- An aircraft must be flown at least 1,000ft above the highest obstacle within 5 nautical miles of the estimated position of the aircraft, except that, if the aircraft is at 3,000ft or below, it must be clear of cloud and in sight of the surface.
- In controlled airspace, the aircraft must be flown at the appropriate semicircular level unless authorised by ATC.
- Outside controlled airspace, the aircraft must be flown at a level that is in accordance with the quadrantal rule, unless the flight is at 3,000ft or below.

Other rules will also apply, depending on the type of airspace, regarding flight plans, keeping a listening watch and complying with ATC instructions.

Night Flights

When flying at night, VFR flights are not permitted. Therefore, a pilot who wishes to fly at night in VMC in uncontrolled airspace must follow the Instrument Flight Rules.

The rules also require a pilot flying at night to have a 'night rating' or an instrument rating.

Special VFR (SVFR)

If a pilot is unable to fly in accordance with the Instrument Flight Rules in a control zone, ATC may authorise him to do so, provided the traffic conditions and the controller's workload allow this to be done safely.

The pilot must at all times remain clear of cloud and in sight of the surface, and comply with ATC instructions.

ATC will not normally issue a Special VFR clearance to an aircraft intending to depart from an aerodrome within a control zone if the visibility is 1,800 metres or less, and/or the cloud ceiling is less than 600ft.

ATC will provide standard separation between all SVFR flights and other IFR flights.

Other rules of the air still apply.

Within the London Terminal Area, special lanes exist in which VFR flights are handled under the Special VFR conditions.

Military Flights
Military Aerodrome
Traffic Zones (MATZ)

These protect the immediate vicinity of military airfields, extending from ground level to specified upper limits.

Military Training
Areas (MTAs)

These are blocks of airspace designed for the training and practice of military traffic. When such danger areas are 'active' civil traffic is prohibited from entering them. It is common for many of these areas not to be used during the night or at weekends and aircraft may then be permitted to cross under ATC surveillance. In addition, some airways cross training areas but restrictions are placed on their use by specifying limitations as to times of operation, for example by limiting their availability to 'weekends only' or by placing time limits on their periods of use. There are also Air-to-Air Refuelling Areas (AARA), Areas of Intense Air Activity (AIAA) and Aerial Tactics Areas (ATA). A Danger Area Crossing and Activity Information Service is available to pilots on a variety of VHF and UHF frequencies.

Military Flying

Anybody who listens to military pilots and their respective ground controllers will soon realise that their messages are fewer, more abrupt and concise, and more difficult to understand without some degree of practice.

Military pilots are not as restricted as their civilian colleagues since they must obviously be able to operate in a responsive and flexible environment as part of their operational needs.

Military transport flights do often use the normal airways system when they will be under the control of the civil air traffic

Iberia Airlines Airbus A320. Author

control units with the normal requirements thus imposed, but military controllers at air traffic control centres or military airfields handle the remaining aircraft.

Long-range routes do exist for use by the military, known as Tacan (Tactical Area Navigation) routes; they are indicated on Royal Air Force charts.

Callsigns used by military flights are more difficult to follow, since coded details are often used as well as 'studs' when changing frequency. By reference to a stud or button on the aircraft radio, the pilot can rapidly transfer from one frequency to another without having to select the individual digits, a method very similar to a push-button radio. Consequently the change of frequency is often referred to by the appropriate stud number rather than quoting the actual frequency; therefore the listener can find it difficult to follow radio frequency changes.

There are seven military radar areas, with UHF radio being used for most communication purposes, although military controllers are able to select VHF when talking to pilots who do not have UHF. This happens mostly when military controllers are providing a Middle Airspace or Lower Airspace service to civilian pilots. Specialist publications are available which cover military activity in detail.

Military Traffic Categories

Military air traffic falls into one of two categories — General Air Traffic (GAT) and Operational Air Traffic (OAT).

■ General Air Traffic: The definition for GAT is that flights are conducted in accordance with the regulations and procedures for flight laid down by the civilian aviation authorities and operating under the same procedures as civilian air traffic.

■ Operational Air Traffic: This term refers to flights that are under the control of a military air traffic control authority.
It is possible for GAT traffic to become OAT traffic (or vice versa) as the flight transfers from one type of airspace to the other.

Military Air Traffic Services

Military air traffic which intends to fly as Operational Air Traffic in the London, Scottish or Irish FIRs is required to file a flight plan (or contact the appropriate radio frequency in advance of entering the area) so that the appropriate clearance can be given.

Air France British Aerospace BAe146. Author

Airways Crossing

Aircraft wishing to cross the civilian airways must do so under the radar control of an air traffic control unit; the initial radio call to the radar unit is to be made at least 5 minutes prior to entering controlled airspace.

Aircraft not under radar control (ie operating under a procedural service) are required to file a flight plan and obtain clearance to cross the airway at least 10 minutes before the crossing is commenced.

Only in an emergency may these rules be relaxed. In such cases the aircraft, which will be flying at a level in whole thousands of feet, is to climb 500ft before entering the airway. After the crossing has been completed the aircraft must resume the previous level.

Since military traffic is often required to cross airways, the most frequently used crossings have been established as either Airways Crossing Slots or Radar Video Corridors, at specified levels and widths.

Pilots still need to contact London or Scottish Military Radar prior to the crossing but the procedure is simplified

Long-range radar station, Clee Hill. Author

by the fact that a block of airspace has been established for the specific purpose of facilitating the penetration of controlled airspace.

Radar corridors exist at NITON, Valley, SITKO, Lichfield, Daventry, Westcott, Swindon, Scunthorpe and Antrim.

Military Low Flying

The UK military low flying system covers most airspace from the surface to 2,000ft. Built-up areas, controlled airspace, air traffic zones, etc are avoided. Many of the routes are used in one direction only during daylight.

In Scotland, the Highlands Restricted Area provides for special military training in Instrument Meteorological Conditions and is therefore closed to other traffic.

In tactical training areas military jets may fly as low as 100ft above the surface. They operate on the 'see and avoid principle' since radar cover is generally not possible.

Civilian pilots who wish to operate at low level are encouraged to notify the military authorities through the Civil Aviation Notification Procedure (CANP) so that military flights can avoid the area. Details of locations and times are passed to military briefing units prior to flight planning.

The general advice to civil pilots is to fly above 2,000ft above ground level wherever possible, to avoid the height band between 250ft and 1,000ft and to keep a good lookout at all times.

Royal Flights

Whenever a civil or military aircraft carries a member of the Royal Family in the UK, an area of protected airspace is created which is intended to ensure the safety of the Royal Flight throughout its journey.

The designated members of the Royal Family are:
Her Majesty The Queen;
His Royal Highness
Prince Philip, The Duke of Edinburgh;
His Royal Highness The Prince of Wales;
Her Royal Highness
The Duchess of Cornwall;
His Royal Highness
The Duke of York;
His Royal Highness The Earl of Wessex;
Her Royal Highness
The Countess of Wessex;
Her Royal Highness The Princess Royal.
However, it is also possible for other members of the Royal Family and other sovereigns and heads of state to be included. Usually the Royal Flight will be routed along the normal UK airways system and through established control zones, and the airspace will then be declared as Temporary Controlled Airspace or CAS-T.

When it is necessary to depart from controlled airspace, a Temporary Airway, also 10 nautical miles wide, will be established for the flight. Similarly areas around airfields used by a Royal Flight will also be declared as Temporary Control Zones or Temporary Control Areas.

The times allowed for CAS-T are from 15 minutes before the arrival or 30 minutes after the departure of the Royal Flight. The usual radio frequencies are used for a Royal Flight, but special ATC procedures apply to ensure separation from other flights.

Where members of the Royal Family fly by helicopter, a Royal Low Level Corridor will be established, with checkpoints at approximately 20-nautical-mile intervals. A 10-mile zone either side of the helicopter's track is applied to military aircraft, and they must at all times be laterally separated by 5 nautical miles from the Royal Flight, although this may be reduced to 3 nautical miles in certain circumstances.

Daily information on Temporary Controlled Airspace and other flying activities is available on Freephone telephone number 0500 354802.

Special arrangements exist for ensuring the safety of Royal and Selected helicopter flights, and for this purpose the major part of the UK landmass is subdivided into Safeguard Areas, each of which has an associated Safeguard Unit. The units are responsible for the provision of an Air Traffic Service to the flight in transit through the area by making use of all available facilities. The callsigns of Royal Flights identify those which are actually carrying Her Majesty the Queen or other members of the Royal Household.

The callsigns used by Royal Flights are as follows:
■ No 32 (The Royal) Squadron:
'Kittyhawk' followed by a number (and the letter 'R' if a member of the Royal Family is on board).
■ The Queen's Helicopter Flight:
'Rainbow' followed by a number (and the letter 'R' if a member of the Royal Family is on board).
■ Civilian chartered aircraft:
'Sparrowhawk' followed by a number (and the letter 'R' if a member of the Royal Family is on board).

Separation Standards

The prime responsibility of the air traffic controller is the safety of flights under his or her control; in part, the means of ensuring safety relies on keeping aircraft apart by internationally agreed minimum limits, known as Separation Standards. Where traffic is operating in controlled airspace the responsibility for ensuring that separation is achieved rests with the controller.

Standard vertical or horizontal separation is to be provided, except when specified otherwise, between the following:

■ All flights in Class A or Class B airspace;
■ Flights operating under IFR in Class C, D and E airspace;
■ Flights operating under IFR and Special VFR;
■ Flights operating under Special VFR;
■ Participating flights operating under IFR in Class F airspace;
■ Flights operating under IFR in Class G airspace, provided they are being given a service from Approach Controllers;
■ Flights in receipt of a Radar Advisory Service.

In certain situations, if the controller considers the circumstances justify it, the separation minima may be increased. Also, the pilot of an aircraft may request an increase in separation.

The opposite can also apply — separation may be reduced in some cases, as, for example, in the vicinity of an airport, when both aircraft can be seen by the controller, or if the pilot of each aircraft can see the other aircraft and can maintain safe separation.

On advisory routes, the minimum vertical separation of 500ft applies in accordance with the quadrantal rule. Separation of aircraft can be achieved by one of two methods: Vertical Separation and Horizontal Separation.

Vertical Separation

This is where the vertical distance between civilian aircraft is never less than the following minima:

Up to FL290:   1,000ft.
Above FL290:   2,000ft,

except that 1,000ft will be permitted where RVSM* approved aircraft are operating in RVSM airspace (as in the UK).

*RVSM = Reduced Vertical Separation Minima. In UK airspace, RVSM was introduced in April 2001, some nine months ahead of the European implementation date, extending the North Atlantic system of reduced separation. This provided an additional six flight levels (FL300, FL320, FL340, FL360, FL380 and FL400).

Horizontal Separation

There are three types of horizontal separation:
■ Lateral separation;
■ Longitudinal separation;
■ Radar separation.

Lateral Separation Based on Specified Tracks

Lateral separation applies where the distance between aircraft is never less than specified, according to the conditions. These conditions vary between 15 and 30 nautical miles, according to the tracks of the aircraft and their respective distances from radio navigation aids.

Lateral Separation Based on Geographical Positions

Geographical separation must be positively indicated by position reports over different locations, which are specified in the relevant documents as being adequately separated. The separation distance must be constant or increasing.

Longitudinal Separation Based on Time and Distance

This is arranged to ensure that aircraft spacing is never less than the minimum required. For this purpose the controller may require flights to depart from an airfield at specified intervals, to increase or reduce speed to maintain separation, or to hold a following flight over a specific location in order to lose time.

Separation by time varies, according to different circumstances, between 2 minutes and 10 minutes.

The longitudinal separation based on distance also varies considerably, but can be reduced to 5 nautical miles in certain circumstances.

Radar Separation

Horizontal separation using radar applies to most flights using controlled airspace. The separation may be as low as 3 miles, when both aircraft are operating in lower airspace, and when authorised by the CAA. In most cases, the minimum is 5 miles, but in some situations it must be increased to 10 miles.

Emergencies

Any pilot in difficulty or in urgent need of help whilst in flight may contact the Distress and Diversion Unit (D and D) at the Scottish, London or Shannon Air Traffic Control Centres on the VHF International Aeronautical Emergency Frequency (121.5MHz VHF and 243.0MHz UHF), which operates on a continuous basis. The callsign is 'Swanwick Centre', 'Scottish Centre' or 'Shannon Centre', as appropriate. When a pilot contacts the D and D cell at either centre the position of the aircraft may be determined by direction-finding equipment located at various stations in the UK.

There are two classes of emergency message:

Distress

A condition of being threatened by serious and/or imminent danger and of requiring immediate assistance. The callsign used by the pilot is 'Mayday, Mayday, Mayday'.

Urgency

A condition concerning the safety of an aircraft or another vehicle, or of some person on board or within sight but which does not require immediate assistance. The callsign in this case is 'Pan-Pan, Pan-Pan, Pan-Pan'. (Note, however, that military pilots only say 'Pan-Pan'.)

Pilots may select the following transponder codes to indicate the emergency situation, or they may be requested to do so by the controller:

■ Aircraft emergency Squawk 7700;
■ Radio failure Squawk 7600;
■ Hijack or other act of violence Squawk 7500.

However, if an aircraft in an emergency is already transponding on an operational code, the pilot will not normally select any of the above codes unless he decides, or is advised, to do so.

Distress Messages

When a distress transmission is received on a frequency other than 121.5MHz, all other transmissions become secondary. The distress transmission is top priority and all other stations on that particular frequency must be silent.

Depending on the circumstances the distress traffic may be requested to change frequency by the controller to 121.5MHz (VHF) or 243.0MHz (UHF).

A feature of the emergency system when either of these frequencies is used is the ability of the distress unit to locate the precise position of the aircraft in trouble very quickly by means of an auto-triangulation system. Direction-finding equipment based at Birmingham, Cardiff, Gatwick, Heathrow, Manchester, Stansted and nine military airfields provides immediate information to the control centre where the details are instantly displayed on a high-definition VDU which has a database of full-colour Ordnance Survey maps with airfields, navigation aids, radio beacons, etc included. Aircraft are identified by three radio direction fixes and one of the important advantages is that the aircraft does not have to carry a transponder. The auto-triangulation

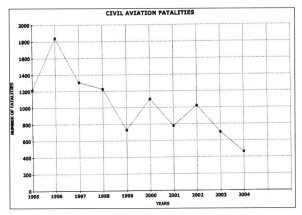

CIVIL AVIATION FATALITIES

2004 saw the lowest ever number of fatalities for civil aviation flights, in spite of the large increase in the number of aircraft flown. (Note that terrorist activities are not included.) ICAO

system is operational in most of central and southern England.

Where possible the following details should be included in the initial transmission:

■ Station being called;
■ Callsign;
■ Aircraft type;
■ Nature of emergency;
■ Intention of the flight;
■ Position, flight level and heading;
■ Number of persons on board.

Pilots are at liberty to call the Distress and Diversion Unit at either London or Scottish Control to practise an emergency situation provided actual emergencies are not affected. In these circumstances the callsign used will be 'Practice Pan' spoken three times.

Airproxes

In 1994 the UK Civil Aviation Authority adopted the ICAO term Airprox to describe incidents which could have safety implications. The definition of Airprox is: 'A situation in which, in the opinion of a pilot or a controller, the distance between aircraft as well as their relative positions and speed have been such that the safety of the aircraft involved was, or may have been, compromised.'

There are four agreed categories:

■ A. Risk of collision — an actual risk of collision existed.
■ B. Safety not assured — the safety of the aircraft was compromised.
■ C. No risk of collision — no risk of collision existed.
■ D. Risk not determined — insufficient information was available to determine the risk involved, or inconclusive or conflicting evidence precluded such determination.

Inevitably, incidents occur which may compromise the safety of air travel, usually caused by errors or unforeseen events somewhere in the system. It is often the case that two or more events occur which combine to create the situation of risk.

A tremendous amount of care and evaluation is exercised in designing, developing and implementing systems and procedures which limit the likelihood of error to a tolerable level. Nevertheless, aviation and air traffic control require a degree of human input and it would be naive to expect such a complex operation to exist without ever involving any incidents. The best that can be achieved is that those occurrences result in a fail-safe rather than a fail-dangerous situation. The perception of risk can mean different things to different people — a pilot flying an aircraft at high speed in busy airspace may well consider the close proximity of another aircraft to be a real threat. Careful analysis later, however, may reveal that safety was not compromised.

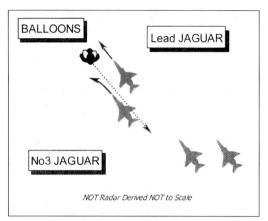

Two examples of Airprox incidents investigated by the UK Airprox Board in 2003.
UKAB

BALLOONS

Lead JAGUAR

No3 JAGUAR

NOT Radar Derived NOT to Scale

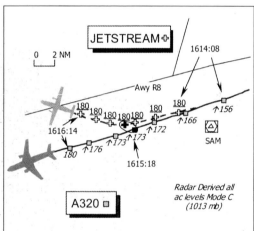

JETSTREAM ✛

1614:08

0   2 NM

Awy R8

180 180 180 180180   180   180
180 180 180 180180   180   ↑156
1616:14   ↑166
                    ↑172
                    △   SAM
    180 ↑173↑173
    ↑176 ↑173
1615:18

*Radar Derived all
ac levels Mode C
(1013 mb)*

A320 ▫

Incidents are investigated by the UK Airprox Board, an independent organisation sponsored jointly by the Civil Aviation Authority and the Ministry of Defence. There are eight civilian and six military members (all volunteers) and a chairman. Their expertise covers all aspects of civil and military aviation and air traffic control.

The sole objective of any investigation is to enhance flight safety by identifying the reasons for the incident and to take steps to ensure, as far as possible, that the situation does not occur again. It is not the purpose of the board to apportion blame or liability; therefore the names of companies and individuals involved are not included in the reports.

Detailed painstaking and impartial investigation of such occurrences has to be available for the purpose of learning from the failings of humans, machines and working practices so that, where appropriate, modifications can be introduced in an attempt to eliminate similar situations in the future. The public notion of incidents in the air is described in the media by the emotive term 'near miss'. In fact, the correct description of Airprox covers all incidents investigated by the board.

The number of Airprox incidents reported by pilots and controllers has steadily fallen over the last 10 years. The latest Airprox report, covering the first half of 2004, shows that although the number of reports increased, compared with 2000 to 2003, only eight were classed as risk category A, and none of these involved civil transport aircraft.

2. Radiotelephony

Communication Systems

Communications between aircraft in flight and ground-based control centres, and between separate ground facilities, are achieved by one of two methods.

The first is the Aeronautical Mobile Service (AMS), which covers communications between the ground and aircraft, dealing with all messages necessary to ensure the safety of flight. This may be through voice transmissions or data transfer.

Secondly, the Aeronautical Fixed Service (AFS) is concerned with the worldwide relaying of messages between various ground stations that are concerned with all aspects of aviation. One of the most important components of this service is the Aeronautical Fixed Telecommunications Network or AFTN. This is a network joining all units concerned with aviation (airports, airlines, control centres, weather centres and the like), each with a unique coded address, which permits a message generated anywhere within the system to be routed worldwide.

Radio Communication

The International Civil Aviation Organisation (ICAO) is responsible for radiotelephony (RT) phraseology

Control tower, Southampton airport. Author

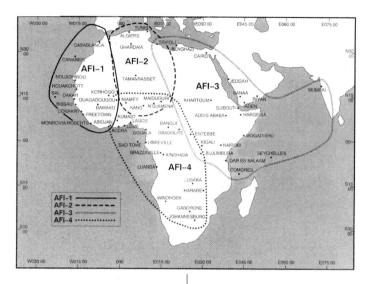

High-frequency radio coverage, Africa. Reproduced by kind permission of the OC No 1. AIDU

procedures which are generally followed by all aviation authorities, although individual states may vary some of the procedures because of local circumstances. These procedures are described and illustrated in documents issued by ICAO and the relevant state aviation authorities.

The main international publication for RT phraseology is the ICAO document PANS-RAC Doc 4444 ('Procedures for Air Navigation Services — Rules of the Air and Air Traffic Services'), which is part of the publication *Procedures for Air Navigation Services — Air Traffic Control*, originally prepared by the Air Traffic Control Committee of the International Conference on North Atlantic Route Service Organisation in Dublin in 1946.

Another important document is the ICAO *Manual of Radiotelephony* (Document 9432 — AN/925), which contains examples of phraseology in common use in air traffic control. It is a lengthy publication which covers numerous situations encountered in ATC; the examples are shown clearly by a system of illustrated diagrams. In the

foreword to the manual the importance of great care in radio procedures is stressed: 'constant attention to correct and concise phraseology and proper procedures at all times will result in their becoming automatic which can only raise the general level of quality of aeronautical radiotelephony and consequently improve the safety of operations both in the air and on the ground'.

In the UK, the Civil Aviation Authority publishes its *Aeronautical Information Publication* (often referred to by its original title, the *Air Pilot*), which sets out the variations (known as 'differences') to the ICAO procedures.

There are two publications which cover radiotelephony procedures in the UK: the primary source of information is the detailed *Manual of Air Traffic Services* (CAP 493), together with a handbook entitled the *Radiotelephony Manual* (CAP 413).

Both these documents, including any new changes, can be accessed on the internet through the Civil Aviation Authority website at www.caa.co.uk under 'Publications', or alternatively they can be purchased from Documedia Solutions.

Throughout this book the examples quoted follow the procedures quoted in the above publications unless stated otherwise.

Use of English

The English language is used throughout the world for international air traffic control messages. It is essential that aircrew and controllers, especially those who do not use English as their first language, adopt and follow agreed procedures to ensure that phrases and words are clearly understood.

Obviously, the correct interpretation of ATC procedures is of vital importance if misunderstandings are to be avoided. There have been (and still are) numerous examples of risk-bearing situations, and worse, which have been found to been partially the result of the careless use of RT phraseology.

Surprisingly, in spite of this evidence, pilots often fail to follow some of the basic rules and have to be corrected by controllers. In the UK, it is very unusual for controllers to use unconventional language or procedures.

In countries where English is not the first language, the national tongue is normally used by ATC for internal flights, even though the aircraft may be under the control of a centre dealing with international flights. For example, the pilot of an Air France flight between Paris and Nice will almost certainly use the French language throughout the trip. In fact, a recent attempt by Air France to require its pilots to speak English at all times had to be hastily withdrawn when strike action was threatened.

British Airways Boeing 757. *British Airways*

The Phonetic Alphabet

In order to standardise the use of the English language, the alphabet is represented phonetically in accordance with the following list. Whenever clarification is required words are spelled out using this alphabet.

Letter	Word	Pronunciation
A	Alpha	AL FAH
B	Bravo	BRAH VOH
C	Charlie	CHAR LEE
D	Delta	DELL TAH
E	Echo	ECK OH
F	Foxtrot	FOKS TROT
G	Golf	GOLF
H	Hotel	HOH TELL
I	India	IN DEE AH
J	Juliett	JEW LEE ETT
K	Kilo	KEY LOH
L	Lima	LEE MAH
M	Mike	MIKE
N	November	NO VEM BER
O	Oscar	OSS CAH
P	Papa	PAH PAH
Q	Quebec	KEH BECK
R	Romeo	ROW ME OH
S	Sierra	SEE AIR RAH
T	Tango	TANG GO
U	Uniform	YOU NEE FORM
V	Victor	VIK TAH
W	Whiskey	WISS KEY
X	X-ray	ECKS RAY
Y	Yankee	YANG KEY
Z	Zulu	ZOO LOO

Numerals are pronounced in accordance with the following table:

0	ZE-RO
1	WUN
2	TOO
3	TREE
4	FOW-er
5	FIFE
6	SIX
7	SEV-en
8	AIT
9	NIN-er

Numbers involving altitude, height, cloud height, visibility and runway visual range which contain whole hundreds and whole thousands are to be transmitted by pronouncing the number of hundreds or thousands separately by the words 'Hundred' or 'Tousand', for example: 'Climb to altitude two tousand five hundred feet,' or 'The runway visual range for runway two seven left is one tousand five hundred metres.'

The digits are spoken separately when referring to callsigns, altimeter settings, flight levels (except Flight Levels 100, 200, 300, and 400) headings, wind speeds, wind direction, transponder squawk codes and radio frequencies, for example: 'Speedbird two zero four six, contact London on one two seven decimal four two,' or 'Easy four one three, squawk two six seven seven.'

References to time are normally given using minutes only, except where there could be some confusion. Again, the digits are spoken separately, for example: 'Jersey two four two, your approved departure time is now two three,' or 'Lufthansa one six two estimating TALLA at four eight.'

Where decimals are involved, the word is pronounced 'Day See Mal', eg 'One Three Five Decimal Six'. However, in practice, the word decimal is frequently omitted, particularly where radio frequencies are involved. In this case, for example, it would be: 'One Three Five Six'.

Priorities

Messages are classified into types and priorities, as set out below:

- 1st priority — Distress messages, identified by the prefix 'Mayday', spoken three times;

- 2nd priority — Urgent messages, identified by the prefix 'Pan-Pan' spoken three times;

- 3rd priority — Messages concerning direction finding;

- 4th priority — Flight safety messages, including ATC messages and position reports;

- 5th priority — Messages concerning meteorology;
- 6th priority — Flight regularity messages (known as 'company messages').

Transmissions

Pilots of aircraft under the jurisdiction of a particular controller will be able to hear the transmissions from that controller, and also transmissions from all other aircraft in the area on the same frequency.

Before attempting to establish contact with a controller, therefore, the pilot must listen on the particular frequency to check that no other transmissions are taking place. Once this is reasonably certain the pilot will attempt to contact the controller. Most pilots include relevant information about their flight as part of their first transmission on each new frequency, without waiting to check if the controller is actually receiving the message, for example: 'London, good morning, Shamrock one five nine passing Flight Level one two zero cleared Flight Level one five zero, heading two eight five.'

In the event of a failure to make contact, the pilot will return to the last frequency on which successful transmissions were made and explain that no contact can be established. The controller will then check with the next sector and possibly give the pilot an alternative radio frequency.

The 'readability' (ie the clarity of transmissions) is expressed in accordance with the following scale:
- Readability 1 — Unreadable;
- Readability 2 — Readable now and then;
- Readability 3 — Readable but with difficulty;
- Readability 4 — Readable;
- Readability 5 — Perfectly readable.

Communication Services

There are three kinds of aeronautical communication services:
- Air Traffic Control, using licensed ATC officers who are regulated by the Civil Aviation Authority;
- Flight Information Service at aerodromes, which can be provided only by licensed flight information service officers (FISOs) who are regulated by the Civil Aviation Authority. The callsign used is 'Information';
- Air/Ground Communications at aerodromes, provided by unlicensed radio operators who have a certificate of competency for radio operations from the Civil Aviation Authority. The callsign used is 'Radio'.

Icelandair Boeing 757s. Icelandair

FISOs at aerodromes may pass instructions to aircraft and other vehicles on the ground, but information only to aircraft in flight. For example, to indicate that there is nothing to prevent an aircraft taking-off, the phrase 'take-off at your discretion' will be used. Air/Ground operators, however, are not permitted to use the expression 'at your discretion'.

Information passed to an aircraft by a FISO is to be acknowledged by the use of the callsign or the word 'roger' and the callsign. Pilots shall notify FISOs or Radio Operators before changing frequency. In controlled airspace, however, changes of frequency will be given by the controller.

Clearances and other messages are to be spoken reasonably slowly since they may have to be written down by one of the crew. Where a clearance originates from another unit, this will be stated in the message; eg 'London Control clears you to . . .'

Messages transmitted from aircraft should refer at the start of the broadcast to the designation of the service being called. The main control centres for the UK are London and Scottish, and messages for these centres are prefixed 'London Control' and 'Scottish Control' respectively. In practice it is usual for the full title to be used only on first contact, after which they are commonly referred to as 'London' and 'Scottish'. In Irish airspace the equivalent centre is at Shannon, with the callsign 'Shannon Control'.

Aerodrome control messages are prefixed with the name of the aerodrome and the type of service. For example, 'Heathrow Approach', 'Manchester Ground', 'Gatwick Delivery' etc. Information service messages are preceded by the name of the service, eg 'London Information', or 'Scottish Information'.

Air Traffic Service Units (ATSUs) are identified by the following suffixes:
■ Aerodrome Control 'Tower'
■ Ground Movement Control 'Ground'
■ Ground Movement Planning 'Delivery'
■ Approach Control 'Approach'
■ Radar (in general) 'Radar'

A typical ATC transmitter mast. Author

- Approach Radar Control
  'Arrival/Departure' ('Radar' when combined)
- Precision Approach Radar Control
  'Talk down'
- Area Control 'Control'
- Flight Information 'Information'

Aircraft Callsigns

Most civil transport aircraft which are heard on airband radios have callsigns allocated by the airline company concerned, together with a flight number. In many cases the first part of the callsign will be the actual name of the airline.

However, there are several which do not comply with this general rule, the most common being 'Speedbird', the callsign for all British Airways aircraft, with the exception of the internal Shuttle flights.

Following the first part of the callsign there will usually be a three- or four-character number or combination of numbers and letters. Many callsigns will have been in use for a considerable time, sometimes for several years.

However, many airlines, including BA, use callsigns which do not include the actual flight number.

For example, BA flights between London Heathrow and Jersey use 16 for all outbound flights and 17 for all inbound flights, followed by a letter. Between Heathrow and Newcastle flights use 12 outbound and 13 inbound. It is therefore quite difficult to determine which route an aircraft is on without this information.

Other types of callsigns are mainly numerical, for example 'N456789'. After using the full callsign on making first contact the flight may then use an abbreviated callsign with the last three digits, eg 'November 789'.

Aircraft without flight numbers are referred to by the aircraft registration which is quoted in full on first contact. For example, G ABCD, on initial contact would be 'Golf Alpha Bravo Charlie Delta'. After contact has been established, and provided there is no risk of confusion with other aircraft, the callsign may be abbreviated to 'Golf Charlie Delta'.

Several airlines use callsigns which combine numbers with a letter code. The numerical element relates to part or all of the timetable number, while the letters are applied as a kind of code that may or may not bear a resemblance to the airports concerned. Sometimes a letter (D for Dublin, for example) follows the numbers as an indication of the route, ie DA indicates an outbound trip, DB an inbound trip.

Many of these callsigns, however, are very difficult to identify and specialist publications are required if there is to be any chance of decoding the information.

Callsign Confusion

The sheer volume of flights operating within Europe today is such that it is inevitable that aircraft with similar, or even identical, parts of the callsign will occur on a particular frequency at the same time. In a perfect world it should be possible to devise a system whereby no two aircraft with similar callsigns would be in the same airspace at the same time, but this has proved to be extremely difficult to achieve, not least because of the limitations of using three or four digits.

Another consideration to be borne in mind is the ease (or otherwise) with which alpha-numeric callsigns can be spoken and understood both by controllers and pilots. There is always a chance of mis-hearing complicated combinations of letters and numbers if they are difficult to say.

It has been regularly observed that callsign confusion can occur simply because of carelessness and lack of attention to correct transmitting technique. Clipped transmissions, blocking of frequencies and failure to follow standard procedures can lead to the wrong aircraft responding to an ATC instruction or alternatively can result in a controller falsely believing a particular flight has correctly responded to a message.

Current thinking on the callsign confusion problem is concentrating on the development of techniques for alerting controllers and pilots to the possibility of a problem and ensuring that the likelihood of misunderstandings is reduced to a tolerable level.

Eventually, when messages are exchanged between control units and aircraft by datalink, the use of unique aircraft identifiers will eliminate the possibility of a message being acted upon by a flight for which it was not intended. Until this day comes, vigilance and care on the part of controllers and pilots is essential, together with careful consideration of which callsigns are easy to use.

First Contact

The initial call, made by en-route traffic entering UK airspace, will establish contact with ATC on the radio frequency given by the previous sector. The same procedure applies when a flight has just departed from an airport. The transfer of control from one air traffic unit to the next will have been co-ordinated, usually by telephone, computer link or standing agreement between the controllers involved, so that the new controller will be fully aware of the flight prior to the transfer taking place.

The first call should be in the following form:

- a. Full callsign of the addressee;
- b. Full callsign of the originator;
- c. The text of the message.

For example:

- a. 'London Control';
- b. 'American three seven';
- c. 'flight level one four zero routing direct to Southampton'.

The 'London' controller at Swanwick will respond by acknowledging the first call and will continue by giving the flight its clearance.

- a. 'American three seven';
- b. 'London Control';
- c. 'Roger, climb flight level three two

zero, route from your present position direct to Land's End.'

More examples are given later.

Readbacks

Certain information given by ATC has to be read back by the pilot to ensure correct receipt and understanding. The messages requiring readback are given in the UK *Aeronautical Information Publication* and details are listed below:

- Level instructions;
- Heading instructions;
- Speed instructions;
- Airways or route clearances;
- Runway-in-use;
- Clearance to enter, land on, take-off, backtrack, cross or hold short of an active runway;
- Squawk code operating instructions;
- Altimeter settings;
- VDF information;
- Frequency changes;
- Type of service.

Controllers are to prompt a pilot if a readback is not immediately forthcoming. Errors in a readback must be corrected by the controller, and the pilot must then read back the corrected version.

Following first contact and the passing of the necessary messages, two-way communication may be continued as required without the need to wait for acknowledgement of each call, although messages may be very much abbreviated. Also, the reference to the ground station callsign may be omitted after satisfactory two-way communication has been established.

As the aircraft approaches the limit of the particular sector, ATC will instruct the flight to change frequency to the next unit specifying the service controller by name. Similar messages will be transmitted when the next frequency concerns another centre (eg Brest, Scottish, Shannon, Shanwick, Maastricht, etc) or airport (eg Heathrow Approach, Manchester, Birmingham, etc) or a radar advisory service (eg London Military). In each case the name of the centre will be given.

Unfortunately, in spite of careful attention to detail in RT procedures, mistakes and misunderstandings do sometimes occur. It has been established that the human mind can play tricks with speech, and pilots and controllers occasionally say words or phrases which are not intended, even though they are convinced that they have acted correctly. It is only when audio tapes are played back that the error can be shown.

Sentences with numerical content, especially when these involve two or three instructions in the same message, are at particular risk. Simple confusion can occur when, for example, a heading is mis-heard as a flight level, eg 'three two zero degrees' is interpreted as 'flight level three two zero', especially if the pilot is anticipating a clearance to that level. All these cases can be avoided by careful attention to correct phraseology.

One of the major factors limiting the capacity of Europe's airspace is the need to pass voice instructions to pilots and to listen to the readbacks to ensure correct interpretation. The correction of errors and misunderstood words creates delay and reduces the limited time available to talk to other flights.

Understanding ATC Transmissions

Although at first it may not appear to be the case, ATC messages follow a logical and carefully organised structure laid down in training, with an almost automatic response to situations, intended to ensure that the sequence of phrases is reliable and consistent. In this section the terms used, and the interpretation of the messages heard every day in the various categories of airspace, are explained.

Firstly, there are some basic rules governing the application of ATC phraseology.

Measurement Systems

ATC language covers an unusual combination of measurement systems, some imperial and some metric, which can be seen by comparing the following:

Units of Measurement used in ATC

Distances used in navigation, position reports, etc, generally in excess of 2 or 3 nautical miles
Nautical miles and tenths, but spoken as 'miles'.

Distance from cloud
Metres

Relatively short distances such as those relating to aerodromes (eg runway lengths, distances of obstructions from runway or of facilities from the aerodrome where accuracy of greater than one-tenth of a nautical mile is required)
Metres

Radar-position reporting and distance from touchdown
Nautical miles and fractions thereof but spoken as 'miles'

Radar-azimuth displacement from final approach track
Metres

Altitudes, elevations and heights
Feet

Depths of snow and slush
Centimetres or millimetres

Horizontal speed including wind speed
Knots

Vertical speed
Feet per minute

Wind direction for landing and taking-off
Degrees magnetic

Wind direction except for landing and taking-off
Degrees true

Visibility
Kilometres and metres

Runway Visual Range
Metres

Altimeter setting
Millibars

Temperature
Degrees Celsius

Weight

Metric tonnes or kilogrammes

Time

Hours and minutes, the day of 24 hours beginning at midnight UTC

The standardisation of international units of measurement is part of the role of the International Civil Aviation Organisation (ICAO). These units cover all areas of airborne and ground-based operations, with the Système International d'Unités, known as SI, as the standard for aviation worldwide. These measurements are essentially metric, although it has been recognised that certain units outside the SI system have a special place in aviation and for that reason have been retained for an indefinite period of time. In the UK, the principal measurements treated as exceptions are the nautical mile, the knot, and the foot when used in relation to levels. There are a number of differences from the ICAO standards, which are to be found in CAA documentation.

Distances

All distances shown on radio navigation charts, usually related to radio beacons or other navigation positions, are referred to in nautical miles. One nautical mile is equal to 6,080ft compared with 5,280ft to a statute mile. The following table may be used to convert nautical miles into statute miles or kilometres:

- Multiply nautical miles by 1.85 to obtain kilometres;
- Multiply nautical miles by 1.15 to obtain statute miles;
- Multiply statute miles by 1.60 to obtain kilometres;
- Multiply statute miles by 0.87 to obtain nautical miles;
- Multiply kilometres by 0.54 to obtain nautical miles;
- Multiply kilometres by 0.62 to obtain statute miles.

Distance Measuring Equipment (DME) carried on board aircraft receives radio transmissions from ground beacons and enables the distance to or from that particular point to be calculated automatically.

Aircraft are therefore able to obtain precise positioning from any beacon within range with this equipment. Messages from ATC often contain references to mileages from reporting points, mainly when restrictions are placed on requirements of ATC. A number of airways intersections, and reporting points, are identified by their relative distances to other land-based navigational beacons, for example: 'Speedbird five one two descend when ready flight level one two zero to be level two zero DME before Lambourne.'

Speed of aircraft is measured in knots (nautical miles per hour). At levels greater than 25,000ft it is not practical to use knots as a measure of speed due to errors caused by low air density, so a comparison relating to the local speed of sound is used instead, known as the Mach number. This means that speed is quoted as a ratio of the speed of sound, after the Austrian physicist Ernst Mach (1838–1916). Most passenger jet aircraft cruise at speeds around Mach 0.8. Cruising speeds are important in flight planning for controllers and the Mach number technique provides a reliable and effective means of ensuring separation. This technique is especially useful for oceanic flights which are beyond the range of radar and rely on accurate speed control as a primary means of ensuring separation. However, the speed of sound is not constant but decreases with a reduction in temperature which occurs with an increase in altitude. For example, it is 660 knots at mean sea level and 589 knots at Flight Level 300.

ATC may require aircraft to comply with certain conditions concerning aircraft speed, either in maintaining a particular speed or by reducing speed to a certain level, for example: 'KLM 481 speed not greater than decimal eight two until advised'. Approaches to airports usually specify maximum speeds, and similarly departures must comply with speed restrictions.

Levels

Three terms are used in air traffic control to describe the vertical distance of an aircraft above the surface of the earth. These are 'flight levels', 'altitude' and 'height'.

Flight Levels

Messages concerning high-flying traffic will be heard to refer to 'flight levels' as two- or three-digit numbers, being the level in thousands of feet with the last two digits omitted. Feet are used as the unit of measurement in most countries, although metres are the unit in China, Russia and other countries of eastern Europe.

For example, 'flight level three seven zero' indicates a flight level of approximately 37,000ft, 'flight level two four zero' is approximately 24,000ft, 'flight level nine zero' is approximately 9,000ft, and so on.

The exceptions to this rule, in UK airspace, are Flight Levels 100, 200, 300 and 400 which are spoken as 'hundreds'. For example, 'flight level three hundred'. This was originally introduced only for FL100, to avoid confusion with FL 110.

Altitude

The term 'altitude' is used to define the vertical position of an aircraft above mean sea level, using the local air pressure setting, which is identified by the letters 'QNH'.

Height

The term 'height' is used to define the vertical position of an aircraft above the surface of the earth (in virtually all cases this will be the actual runway surface) using the airfield air pressure setting which is identified by the letters 'QFE'.

These three terms, and their relationship to air pressure, need to be explained in more detail.

Pressure Variations

The instrument on board an aircraft used to measure its distance above the earth is called the altimeter. This is a device that reacts to atmospheric pressure. Air

JAL Boeing 747. JAL

pressure is greatest at sea level, so as the distance above the earth increases, atmospheric pressure decreases, and this change in pressure can be measured on a scale on the altimeter, calibrated to indicate hundreds and thousands of feet.

The complication for aviation is that atmospheric pressure changes almost constantly, as anyone listening to the daily weather forecast will know. References to areas of 'low pressure' or 'high pressure' are familiar terms, and as the atmospheric pressure changes in different parts of the country so the altimeter reading varies.

This means that aircraft flying at high level would need to have their altimeters adjusted continuously to the local atmospheric pressure to ensure that their level indication is correct. For high-speed traffic, travelling perhaps thousands of miles every day, this would require a whole series of continuous adjustments, dependent upon information provided by ground stations.

If an aircraft is being flown using a pressure setting which is lower than the actual pressure, the aircraft will actually be lower than the level indicated by the instruments. The reverse is also true.

Standard Pressure Settings

This is clearly an impractical and somewhat risky procedure, and it was soon realised that it was essential to develop a method of overcoming this difficulty. The system used worldwide is to specify a theoretical atmospheric pressure, known as the 'Standard Altimeter Setting' (or SPS) of 1013.25 millibars, (or 29.92 inches) irrespective of the actual barometric pressure.

All aircraft above the specified 'Transition Level' (normally in the UK 3,000ft or 6,000ft) have their altimeters set to this standard setting. All aircraft in the same area will then be flying at the same level, with synchronised altimeters. The reading given by the altimeter will, of course, only be correct when the actual pressure is 1013.25; at all other pressures, the level will be more or less than the true level but whether the true setting is 1013.25 millibars or not is irrelevant because as all aircraft are on the same setting, any variation in the actual level will be common to all. By this means proper separation between aircraft is ensured.

In many other countries, principally the USA, pilots do not use millibars but, instead, use inches of mercury. Thus, 29.92 inches is equivalent to 1013.25 millibars. Great care has to be taken by international flight crews who may sometimes confuse the two systems.

QFE and QNH

Below transition altitude, vertical distances are described by two distinct terms, both of which rely on actual barometric pressures for the area in which the aircraft is operating. Air traffic controllers will provide

London Terminal Control Centre, West Drayton, Middlesex. Author

aircraft with two separate barometric pressure settings, known by the abbreviations QFE and QNH. (Pilots sometimes refer to these as 'Fox Echo' and 'November Hotel' respectively.)

QFE is the local atmospheric pressure setting, which, when set on the aircraft's altimeter, will cause the instrument to read zero when the aircraft is on the runway. When this setting is in use, the term used to refer to vertical distance is 'height'.

QNH is also the local atmospheric pressure setting, but when this setting is set on the altimeter, the reading on the aircraft instruments shows feet above mean sea level. This is important for ensuring that aircraft maintain a safe clearance above ground obstructions, hills, mountains and so on. The term used to describe this vertical distance is 'altitude'.

One millibar represents approximately 30ft in height, therefore the difference in millibars between the QFE setting and the QNH setting, multiplied by 30, will give the airfield elevation above mean sea level. For example, if the QFE is given as 997 millibars and the QNH is given as 1012 millibars, the difference (15) multiplied by 30 gives the airfield elevation of approximately 450ft. Thus the difference between QFE and QNH will always be the same for each airport.

The Effect of Pressure Variations

The concept of flight levels, altitude and height resulting from the different definitions of atmospheric pressure is often difficult to grasp, so a practical example may be useful. Flight levels, as previously explained, operate at a standard pressure of 1013.25 millibars, regardless of the actual pressure at the time. The base of the imaginary column of air (Flight Level zero) will only coincide with the mean sea level if the actual pressure is the same (ie 1013.25mb).

Imagine the air pressure on a particular day to be 978 millibars; this is approximately 35 millibars lower than the standard 1013.25mb. Since each millibar is equivalent to a change of approximately 30ft the resulting difference between the actual pressure and the standard pressure is 35 times 30, ie 1,050ft — say 1,000ft for our purposes.

In this example, the mean sea level pressure is 978mb. The theoretical pressure of 1013.25mb is therefore approximately 1,000ft lower than the actual sea level. This means that an aircraft flying with a QNH setting of 978 at 7,000ft would be at the same level as an aircraft flying at FL80 on the standard setting, the pressure difference accounting for the discrepancy in levels.

Flight levels are used above the transition level, while below it, on the QNH setting, references to levels are expressed as altitudes. Great care has to be taken by pilots and controllers where flight levels and altitudes may be confused and there have been numerous examples where aircraft in terminal areas have lost separation for this reason.

For example, aircraft en route to Heathrow normally descend to FL70 in the holding stacks, while departing flights are restricted to a maximum altitude of 6,000ft. When the air pressure is low, as in our example earlier, the lowest flight level for arrivals is raised to FL80 to avoid conflictions.

In the USA the transition level is 18,000ft, much higher than in the UK. American pilots flying in European airspace often refer to levels below 18,000ft in altitudes, instead of the correct terminology of flight levels. Controllers have to be careful to ensure that the pilot corrects the readback in view of the possible confusion and risk if the incorrect pressure setting is used.

Altimeter Setting Regions

The United Kingdom is divided into a number of regions, known as ASRs (Altimeter Setting Regions), each with a name. As aircraft below transition level pass from one ASR to another, the altimeter scale is reset to ensure the altitude is correct for the atmospheric pressure in that area. Controllers are often heard referring to such regions when talking to pilots of low-flying aircraft.

Cross-country flights, operating at low levels outside controlled airspace, use another type of pressure setting, known as the Regional Pressure Setting (or RPS). This is the lowest forecast pressure setting over the next two hours, designed to ensure that the pilot does not fly too low. The RPS will normally be lower than the local airfield QNH; therefore care is needed when changing from one pressure setting to another.

In addition to the separate regions, the country is also divided into four colour-coded areas (Red, Blue, Yellow and Green) for the purpose of assisting pilots who are unsure of their position. If a pilot is uncertain as to which ASR the aircraft is in, the pilot should operate at the minimum safe level published for the colour region.

To summarise:
■ Flight level is when aircraft are on the standard pressure setting of 1013.25 millibars;
■ Altitude is distance above sea level (QNH);
■ Height is distance above the airfield (QFE);
■ The Regional Pressure Setting is the lowest forecast pressure over the next two hours.

Here are some examples of messages:
ATC: '*Golf Delta Foxtrot, the Barnsley Regional Pressure Setting is nine nine eight millibars.*'

ATC: '*Golf Delta Foxtrot, maintain altitude two thousand five hundred feet on the Regional Pressure Setting nine nine two millibars.*'

ATC: '*All stations — the Cotswold Regional is changing on the hour to nine nine six millibars — new Cotswold Regional nine nine six millibars.*'

ATC: '*Speedbird four four two, descend to altitude three thousand feet, QNH one zero zero four millibars.*'

Military Pressure Settings
In 1990 it became established practice not to use QFE for flights operating at military airfields. However, for practical purposes the use of QFE has been reintroduced.

Some flights, particularly US-based, do not use QNH as an atmospheric setting but instead use 'inches of mercury' to indicate the required pressure.

The Q Code
QNH and QFE are examples of the Q code, which originated when radio messages were transmitted in Morse, and a number of terms were simplified by using three-letter codes starting with the letter Q.

Other examples, often heard in ATC transmissions, are:
■ QSY — Change radio frequency (not an official term);
■ QDM — The magnetic heading required to reach a particular station, usually an airfield, with no wind;
■ QDR — The magnetic heading required to track away from a particular station. The reciprocal of QDM;
■ QTE — True bearing from a particular station to an aircraft;
■ QNE — The reading in feet on the altimeter (when the subscale is set to the standard pressure setting of 1013.25 millibars) when the aircraft is on the touchdown end of the runway.

Changes in Level
Several terms are used to denote changes in level. It is obviously important that such terms are used correctly, otherwise confusion and misinterpretation could result. However, many pilots still use unofficial words in relation to levels.

'Climb'
Instructions involving a change to a higher level include the term 'climb'.

'Descend'*
Instructions involving a change to a lower level include the term 'descend'.

'Maintain'
Aircraft remaining at one particular level are said to be 'maintaining' the level.

'Passing'
Aircraft which are descending, or climbing, use the term passing to describe the actual flight level through which the aircraft is 'passing' at the time the message is transmitted.

'Leaving'
Aircraft which have been given clearance to climb (or descend) will notify ATC when they commence the climb (or the descent) by the term 'leaving' (the flight level).

'Reaching'
Aircraft arriving at a cleared flight level will report to ATC using the term 'reaching'.

'Approaching'
If a flight has been cleared to an intermediate level, after which a further clearance can be expected, the phrase

'approaching'
is used, as the flight nears the intermediate level.

Descend
means descend when you are ready, ie at the pilot's discretion.

'Descend now'
means descend as soon as possible.

'Descend immediately'
indicates an urgent situation and descent should be commenced immediately.

My Travel A320. My Travel Airways

Here are some examples of messages:
ATC: '*Swiss two three seven climb flight level three three zero.*'

AC: '*London, Shamrock two eight two passing flight level one two zero, cleared flight level one five zero.*'
ATC: '*Roger, Shamrock two eight two maintain flight level one five zero on reaching.*'
AC: '*Shamrock two eight two is now reaching and maintaining flight level one five zero.*'

ATC: '*Speedbird four six one descend flight level two nine zero initially, expect further descent to flight level two seven zero after passing Honiley.*'

Note: Instructions concerning flight levels do not include the word 'to'. However, instructions concerning altitude or height do include the word 'to' before the word 'altitude' or 'height'.

Also, the first message where altitude or height is concerned has to include the pressure setting. If this is less than 1,000 millibars the word 'millibars' is to be included in the message.

Headings and Tracks
The direction in which an aircraft is flying is known as its heading and is quoted in terms of degrees of the compass, using three figures in all cases. Each digit is spoken separately.

An aircraft flying due east will be on a heading of 090°, due south is 180°, due west is 270° and due north is 360° (often referred to as 'North'). If the controller requires the aircraft to remain on the same heading the correct word to be used is 'continue'.

Radio navigation charts indicate the headings (or bearings) between navigation beacons in degrees. Aircraft flying between such points would normally be on the heading shown on the chart, except when required by ATC to alter course.

When a flight is required by ATC to remain on a particular heading it is then said to be on a 'radar heading', and this must be continued until ATC advises either a new heading or a return to the original track.

When a flight is not on a 'radar heading' (ie one imposed by ATC) it is said to be on 'own navigation'. Messages concerning headings can often be heard, especially during busy periods. Flights may be required to change direction by a specified amount, to stay on a particular heading, or to turn on to a specified heading. Radar headings may only be assigned when flights are under radar control.

When handing over the flight to the next sector, pilots of aircraft on a radar heading are required to inform the new controller.

Some flight crews may be heard to refer to their direction of flight (incorrectly) as 'steering' or 'assigned'.

The 'track' of an aircraft is the path over the ground actually flown — in other words, the actual course after taking into account any deviation or drifting off course caused by the wind.

Here are some examples of messages:
ATC: '*Speedbird six seven six report heading.*'
AC: '*Two seven zero degrees Speedbird six seven six.*'
ATC: '*Roger, Speedbird six seven six continue present heading until advised.*'
AC: '*Continue present heading Speedbird six seven six.*'
(Later)
ATC: '*Speedbird six seven six resume own navigation.*'
AC: '*Resume own navigation Speedbird six seven six.*'

ATC: '*Alitalia one two five turn left one zero degrees and report new heading.*'
AC: '*Roger Alitalia one two five turn left one zero degrees, the new heading will be two nine five degrees.*'
ATC: '*Thank you Alitalia one two five, make that a radar heading.*'
AC: '*Radar heading two nine five degrees Alitalia one two five.*'

ATC messages concerning changes of heading are of two types — one is where an aircraft is required to fly on a specified compass heading, the other is where the aircraft is required to change course by a specified number of degrees.

For example, imagine an aircraft is flying on a heading of 350°. An instruction to turn right 'one five degrees' would put the aircraft onto a heading of 005°. Alternatively, an instruction to turn onto a heading of 'zero one five degrees' would require the pilot to turn right 25°. Pilots and controllers obviously need to be careful about the use of these heading instructions to avoid mistakes.

The Quadrantal Rule

Pilots flying under Instrument Meteorological Conditions outside controlled airspace, above the transition level and below FL245 must adjust their altimeters to the standard setting of 1013.25 millibars and fly in accordance with what is known as the quadrantal rule, which is devised to ensure that aircraft remain clear of each other by at least 500ft.

Under this rule, aircraft flying on magnetic tracks:
■ between 000° and 089°, must be flown at odd thousands of feet;
■ between 090° and 179°, must be flown at odd thousands of feet plus 500ft;
■ between 180° and 269°, must be flown at even thousands of feet;
■ between 270° and 359°, must be flown at even thousands of feet plus 500ft.

Semicircular Cruising Levels

Before April 2001, in the UK within controlled airspace, ICAO semicircular standard cruising levels applied to aircraft above Flight Level 290.

Below Flight Level 290, aircraft heading in an easterly direction (between 0° and 179°) were to be flown at Flight Levels 10, 30, 50, 70, 90, etc up to 290.

At and above 290, the flight levels were 290, 330, 370, 410 etc in multiples of 4,000ft.

Aircraft heading in a westerly direction (180° to 359°) fly at Flight Levels 20, 40, 60, 80, 100 up to 280. Above 280, flight levels were 310, 350, 390, 430 etc in multiples of 4,000ft.

In April 2001, for flights operating in London airspace above Flight Level 290, the Reduced Vertical Separation Minima (RVSM) programme was implemented, permitting for the first time 1,000ft vertical separation. Six new flight levels were introduced.

The new semicircular cruising levels are now as shown in the diagram (below).

In certain circumstances, controllers have discretion to authorise flights to operate at non-standard cruising levels where appropriate.

Time

In aviation, the time system used is Co-ordinated Universal Time, a combination of two other methods of time measurement — Universal Time and International Atomic Time. UTC (the initials are based on the French definition of Co-ordinated Universal Time) is the accepted standard for worldwide time signal broadcasts used for aviation. It is often shortened to 'Universal' by pilots and controllers.

UTC is used internationally as a reference point for aviation, but pilots will continue to refer to 'local' as the time for the particular time zone they happen to be in.

Also, a common term used by some pilots to represent time is the word 'Zulu'. This is used mainly by military controllers and pilots.

In aviation, particularly where long-range journeys are concerned, there is usually no need to refer to hours, and time is normally expressed only in minutes, unless there is likely to be confusion. Transmissions will, therefore, be heard to refer to minutes only, mainly in connection with estimated times for reaching reporting points or for arrivals at destinations. For example: 'Lufthansa two six nine, passing Ottringham this time, estimate Wallasey at five five.'

Weather

A later chapter deals with weather conditions and an explanation of the terms involved, so mention is made here of only a few commonly heard expressions in ATC transmissions. Poor visibility is always a problem for arriving aircraft, and when conditions are unfavourable aircraft will require frequent updates on local conditions in order that a decision on possible diversions can be made.

One common term which is often heard is 'Runway Visual Range' (RVR) which is given in metres for each runway. Runway Visual Range is given as three separate readings — one at the runway threshold, the second at the midpoint position, and the third at the stop end of the runway.

Semi-circular cruising flight levels in upper airspace where Reduced Vertical Separation Minima applies.

SEMI-CIRCULAR FLIGHT LEVELS IN RVSM AIRSPACE	
TRACK IN DEGREES MAGNETIC	
000 – 179 (EASTBOUND)	180 – 359 (WESTBOUND)
FL 410	FL 400
FL 390	FL 380
FL 370	FL 360
FL 350	FL 340
FL 330	FL 320
FL 310	FL 300
FL 290	

El Al Boeing 777. El Al

A second common term to be heard concerns cumulonimbus storm clouds (CB), which can result in severe buffeting of the aircraft. Pilots will always do their best to avoid such clouds, and they can often be heard asking for permission to change course accordingly.

When these conditions prevail across the country many aircraft change course almost constantly as they zigzag along their route. In each of the following examples the pilot is requesting permission to change direction to avoid bad weather:

AC: *'Alitalia six two mike, may we turn left ten degrees to avoid weather?'*

AC: *'Midland one four two may we turn left ten degrees to avoid a build-up?'*

AC: *'Speedbird five one nine may we turn left ten degrees to avoid some Charlie Bravos?'*
ATC: *'Speedbird five one nine left turn approved, advise me when resuming own navigation.'*

Note the use of the word 'approved' rather than 'cleared', which is used when the request is made by the pilot.

The Flight Management Computer System

Most modern aircraft are fitted with flight management computers which allow the flight to navigate precisely without reference to radio beacons; pilots often request direct routeings if they are so equipped.

Messages from ATC relating to clearances involving direct routeings can be heard frequently, particularly during relatively quiet periods.

Self Positioning

Most modern transport aircraft are provided with sophisticated navigation equipment which enables the pilot to select any position by reference to the latitude and longitude of the chosen point. Details of reporting points are stored in the aircraft navigation computer. The aircraft will then route to that particular location independently of any guidance from ATC or ground-based navigation beacons. This procedure is now quite popular, especially when used to route direct, for example, to the extended centreline of an airport's landing runway. The terms used are 'self positioning' or alternatively 'centre fix' and these can be heard in ATC transmissions fairly regularly.

Although not an officially recognised ATC procedure, its existence is acknowledged by the ATC authorities and some guidance for its use has been issued by the Civil Aviation Authority. The problem is that when a pilot is under radar control or in receipt of an advisory service, a request to 'self position' places the flight in a situation where the ATC unit no longer has total control of the flight and may not be able to provide guidance with regard to terrain clearance and collision avoidance. Neither term has a precise agreed meaning in ATC terms; therefore aircraft crews are required to ensure safe altitudes and to remain inside regulated airspace. They should also recognise that flight management systems are not certificated for use as an aid for instrument approaches, and that each approach is unique.

Traffic Information

References to other aircraft are often heard in ATC transmissions advising a particular flight of other traffic in the area. It is common practice to use a conventional clock system as a means of reference, in preference to compass bearings, where 12 o'clock indicates a position dead ahead.

The inclusion of the word 'company' in the message indicates that the other aircraft is operated by the same airline.

Secondary Surveillance Radar (SSR)

Conventional (or primary) radar relies on the reflected signal from a 'target' — for example, an aircraft — which is received by the radar antenna and displayed on the controller's radar screen. The range of primary radar is limited by the strength of the signal from the ground-based transmitter and consequently the reflection back to the ground receiver. Obviously, the greater the distance between the transmitter and the aircraft, the weaker the reflection.

Secondary surveillance radar, however, differs from primary radar in that the signal transmitted by the ground station is received by the aircraft via equipment on the flightdeck — the transponder — which then transmits a response back to the ground station. The power required to produce a return signal is therefore far less with secondary radar than with primary radar, which depends only on a reflected signal. Consequently, secondary radar has a much greater range than primary radar.

In addition, whilst primary radar displays the position of the aircraft target, secondary radar is capable of interrogating the various systems on the flightdeck and having those details transmitted back to the radar screen at a control centre or airport.

Commercial aircraft flying in Class A or Class B airspace must be operating a transponder which has an additional facility, Mode C (or Mode Charlie), which can be interrogated in more detail.

Before the aircraft departs on a flight in controlled airspace, a flight plan has to be submitted. This plan gives detailed information on the routeing, aircraft type, callsign, etc and this information will be fed into the ATC computer system, together with a four-figure identification number which will relate only to that flight whilst in UK airspace. Many airlines provide scheduled service details weeks or months in advance and the information is stored in the system until the day of the flight. The four-figure code number is known as the 'squawk', and this word is part of the everyday language of air traffic control.

Squawk codes consist of the numbers 0 to 7, meaning that there is a theoretical total of 4,096 codes available for use. With daily European traffic figures now in the region of 30,000, each code has to be reissued seven or eight times each day. This is creating significant logistical problems for the computer systems, and misreading of information by the radar equipment is on the increase. More sophisticated facilities are urgently needed, a subject that is dealt with later in the book.

A flight in controlled airspace, having been allocated a particular squawk number as part of the ATC clearance, will be required to select the appropriate code on the aircraft's transponder. A selective signal from the ground radar station will be transmitted to the aircraft, whereupon the transponder will process the signal and return the transmission to the radar station. This will include the four-figure squawk code.

The information is routed through the ATC computer, where the squawk code is linked to the stored flight plan. Included with the signal are details of the flight level and the attitude of the aircraft (ie climbing or descending). When the computer has sorted the data the radar signal is then passed to the radar controller's screen, which displays the aircraft position, its flight level, an arrow indicating whether the aircraft is in the climb or the descent, and the cleared flight level. The destination may also be shown.

When first contacting a control centre, the pilot is usually requested to squawk 'ident' by operating an identity button which causes the particular radar return to increase in intensity or to flash on the screen.

Squawk codes can be used for several other situations to provide ATC with invaluable information on the progress of the flight. Code 7700, for example, is the code used to denote an emergency on-board condition. Code 7600 indicates radio failure, while code 7500 warns the controller of some unlawful interference with the flight.

The squawk of 7000, known as the 'conspicuity code', is used by aircraft — usually General Aviation (light aircraft) — which are operating outside controlled airspace. Aircraft with radio problems may be asked by ATC to squawk ident if the transmissions are being received, thus indicating to the ground that radio reception is functioning, even if the transmitter on the aircraft is not.

One important safety feature of the transponder is the detection of the actual level being flown. If the pressure subscale on the altimeter has been set incorrectly the controller will be able to observe that the aircraft's actual level varies from the cleared level. A number of potentially dangerous incidents have been avoided through the use of this facility.

A further development in the use of secondary surveillance radar is the ability of transponders to not only pass information to the ground but to question transponders fitted to other aircraft in the vicinity, thereby obtaining independently the details of those flights which might be on a potentially conflicting course.

This system, the Airborne Collision Avoidance System (ACAS), of which the only approved version is the Traffic Alert and Collision Avoidance System (TCAS), is now mandatory in America and Europe for most transport flights.

Because of its significance, further details regarding TCAS are given in the chapter on the Überlingen mid-air collision.

Transmissions

The following section contains a selection of ATC broadcasts and aircraft responses, covering a variety of different circumstances. It does not include messages concerning oceanic clearances, airport arrivals and departures or 'company' messages. All these can be found elsewhere in the book. By reading through these messages, it should be possible to become acquainted in a fairly short time with many of the procedures being used in ATC today, and they will enable the complete beginner to recognise phrases and technical terms.

These examples assume that the flights are under radar control.

Position Reports

The following items of information may be included in the report from the pilot, although, in practice, reports often consist of the callsign and flight level only:

- Aircraft callsign;
- Position;
- Time;
- Level;
- Next position;
- Estimated time of arrival.

Here are some examples of messages:

AC: '*London Control, this is Air Canada eight seven four approaching EVRIN this time, flight level three seven zero, estimating NUMPO at four three.*'
ATC: '*Air Canada eight seven four, London, good morning, maintain flight level three seven zero, route upper lima six zero seven for Frankfurt. Squawk ident on five four seven zero.*'
AC: '*Roger, maintain flight level three seven zero, ident five four seven zero, upper lima six zero seven, Frankfurt, Air Canada eight seven four.*'

Note that the initial contact between the pilot and each sector controller specifies the ATC unit being called. Also, position reports are normally given only on first contact with an ATC unit.

Mach Number Speed Control

ATC: '*KLM seven three five, London, what is your Mach number?*'
AC: '*Mach decimal eight two, KLM seven three five.*'
ATC: '*Roger — break — Lufthansa eight one six four, what is your Mach number?*'
AC: '*Eight one, Lufthansa eight one six four.*'
ATC: '*Roger, Lufthansa eight one six four, speed not greater than decimal eight one.*'

Shanwick Oceanic Control Planning Officer.
Shanwick OCC

AC: 'Speed not greater than decimal eight one Lufthansa eight one six four.'
ATC: 'KLM seven three five speed not less than decimal eight two.'
AC: 'Roger not less than eight two, KLM seven three five. We have the other aircraft in sight at three o'clock.'
ATC: 'KLM seven three five, understood.'

Conflicting Traffic

AC: 'Midland seven kilo echo passing flight level two seven zero for two nine zero — may we continue to three three zero?'
ATC: 'Midland seven kilo echo, negative, maintain flight level two nine zero on reaching — there is crossing traffic at three three zero, left to right, on upper lima nine. Expect further climb in fifteen miles.'

Part of the Controlled Airspace over central England used in the London Control Simulator. DM Aviation / Dale McLoughlin

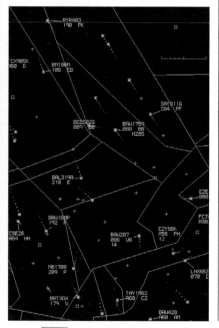

AC: 'Roger, understood Midland seven kilo echo — looking.'
AC: 'Midland seven kilo echo, traffic in sight.'
ATC: 'Roger seven kilo echo.'
(Later)
ATC: 'Midland seven kilo echo, London, well clear of the traffic now, climb flight level three three zero.'
AC: 'Climb flight level three three zero Midland seven kilo echo, thank you. Leaving flight level two nine zero now.'

ATC: 'Golf Charlie Delta traffic information for you, a Cessna one five two in your two o'clock, range seven miles, crossing from right to left similar level.'
AC: 'Golf Charlie Delta roger, traffic in sight.'

ATC: 'United One, London, traffic information is a company Boeing triple seven in your ten o'clock, range twelve miles, crossing left to right under my control, one thousand feet below your level.'
AC: 'United One, roger, we are presently in cloud, but we can see him on TCAS.'

Radar Headings

AC: 'Shuttle seven sierra, good morning leaving flight level nine zero for one three zero, radar heading one eight zero.'
ATC: 'Shuttle seven sierra, good morning continue on the heading, climb flight level two six zero.'
AC: 'On the heading, climb flight level two six zero, Shuttle seven sierra.'
ATC: 'Shuttle seven sierra, are you avoiding weather?'
AC: 'Negative Shuttle seven sierra.'
ATC: 'Shuttle seven sierra, roger, turn left onto a radar heading of one seven zero.'
AC: 'Radar heading one seven zero, Shuttle seven sierra.'

Direct Routeings

AC: 'London control, Kestrel nine nine four, good evening, flight level three five zero, four two DME from Berry Head, for Glasgow.'

ATC: '*Kestrel nine nine four, London, good evening, maintain flight level three five zero, upper november eight six four for Glasgow, squawk ident on three four two two.*'

AC: '*Ident on three four two two, standard for Glasgow, maintain flight level three five zero, Kestrel nine nine four. Any chance of Berry Head direct to the Golf Oscar Whiskey?*'

ATC: '*Kestrel nine nine four, stand by.*'

(Later)

ATC: '*Kestrel nine nine four route from your present position direct to the Golf Oscar Whiskey.*'

AC: '*Direct to the GOW Kestrel nine nine four, thanks very much.*'

North Atlantic Entry

AC: '*London control, Alitalia six zero four good day approaching LIZAD flight level three eight zero.*'

ATC: '*Alitalia six zero four, good morning, maintain flight level three eight zero, route upper lima seven three nine to GAPLI for Kennedy. Do you have your Oceanic clearance?*'

AC: '*Affirm, Alitalia six zero four, it's track Charlie at three eight zero, the entry point is DINIM.*'

ATC: '*Roger, Alitalia six zero four, confirm that you expect to enter the Oceanic area not before time five five?*'

AC: '*Affirm, six zero four. Understand GAPLI not before five five — we are reducing speed to lose time.*'

ATC: '*That's understood, Alitalia six zero four.*'

Turbulence

ATC: '*Britannia two three eight alpha, there is a seven four seven at your flight level crossing left to right about thirty miles ahead — caution turbulent wake.*'

AC: '*OK Sir we can see the traffic — thanks for the warning.*'

AC: '*Baby four zero zero four, London we are experiencing moderate turbulence at flight level three six zero — have you had any previous reports?*'

ATC: '*Negative Baby four zero zero four, that's the first report I've had — do you wish to descend?*'

AC: '*Affirm, Baby four zero zero four.*'

ATC: '*Roger Baby four zero zero four, descend now flight level three four zero.*'

AC: '*Cleared flight level three four zero Baby four zero zero four — leaving three six zero now — thank you.*'

(Later)

AC: '*Baby four zero zero four, reaching flight level three four zero — the turbulence has smoothed out now.*'

ATC: '*Roger Baby four zero zero four.*'

Miscellaneous

AC: '*London, New Zealand two, we have parallel traffic on TCAS at 15 miles — can you tell us his intentions?*'

ATC: '*New Zealand two London it's an Air France Airbus, under my control, just about to start descent to FL230 — no conflict expected.*'

AC: '*New Zealand two thanks for that.*'

ATC: '*Britannia two nine four bravo, London, Birmingham will accept you at flight level eight zero, with no delay, descend now flight level eight zero and route direct to Honiley. It will be a Radar Advisory Service once you leave controlled airspace.*'

AC: '*Roger, direct to Honiley, descend flight level eight zero, expect Radar Advisory outside controlled airspace, Britannia two nine four bravo.*'

Other examples of different situations appear in the appropriate chapters.

3. Tragedy at Überlingen

On 1 July 2002, at 21.35 hours UTC, a Tupolev Tu-154M passenger jet and a Boeing 757 cargo plane collided above the town of Überlingen, Germany, a few kilometres north of Lake Constance. All 60 passengers and 11 crew on the aircraft were killed.

The aircraft had been under the control of Skyguide, the Swiss air navigation organisation, operating from the Zürich Air Traffic Control Centre.

This chapter describes the events leading up to the collision and the findings of the subsequent inquiry.

Airborne Collision Avoidance System (ACAS)

The actions regarding the use of the Airborne Collision Avoidance Systems carried on board both aircraft were a significant factor contributing to the collision; therefore a description of the operating principles will help in understanding the events immediately prior to the time of impact.

ACAS is a 'last resort' safety system, entirely independent of ground-based facilities, in which radio transmissions between aircraft are used to predict possible conflicts. In such situations the system provides instructions in a vertical direction to the crews of the respective aircraft to enable them to avoid each other.

The design of the equipment ensures that the instructions are always generated to provide opposite direction advice for the aircraft involved.

ACAS was developed in the USA, in response to a number of mid-air collisions in its airspace in the 1970s and 1980s. It is intended to prevent such critical situations independently of the normal ATC operation. The only approved system is produced by Honeywell, known as the Traffic Alert and Collision Avoidance System, or TCAS. The latest version of this equipment, Version 7, was fitted to both aircraft involved in the collision at Überlingen, and both systems were in proper working order.

The system is intended to provide avoidance advice where the normal air traffic control process has failed. As the communications are between the conflicting aircraft, the advice will be more accurate than that being received from ground control since the operating principles of the secondary radar inevitably result in a delay in updating the information on the screen. The picture seen by the controller will be several seconds out of

Flight Progress Strips for the two aircraft involved in the mid-air collision at Überlingen.

DHX611	7524	260	360	ABE	KUD	LOK
	0463			2120	2130	2135
LIME TGO	EBBR	320				
B752	465 48		R360			

BTC2937	7520	360	350	NEG	TRA	BEN
	4125			2136	2142	2151
UUDD NINTU	LEBL					
T154	470 44		R360			

date; therefore in an emergency situation any control decisions might make the situation worse.

The 'target' aircraft are presented on the TCAS display as blue or white aeroplane-shaped symbols, each pointing in the direction of flight. Traffic which is non-intrusive (that is, the horizontal distance and/or the vertical separation exceeds the minima required) is shown as a hollow diamond but non-intruding flights which are within six nautical miles and 1,200ft above or below the aircraft are known as 'proximate' aircraft, and are indicated by a solid blue or white diamond.

The pilots of the aircraft are provided with information regarding the relative positions of any proximate flights, indicating their distances, directions and vertical positions. This information is presented to the pilots on a small screen, firstly as a 'Traffic Advisory' (TA), with an aural message 'Traffic, traffic'.

If the threat aircraft continues to intrude into the protected zone around the threatened aircraft, the system generates a further message, known as a 'Resolution Advisory' (RA), accompanied by another aural message advising the pilots of the vertical manoeuvres required to resolve the conflict.

However, the aircraft generating the TA or RA may not, in fact, be the closest aircraft. For example, an aircraft which is 1,000ft below, travelling in the opposite direction, will not generate a warning as it passes underneath. However, a TA will be triggered by another aircraft, 20 miles away, at or approaching the same level and converging.

Around the perimeter of the TCAS display, a red arc indicates a range of vertical speeds that the pilot is expected to avoid in order to comply with the RA. Adjoining this, the arc changes to green, indicating the vertical speed required by the pilot in response to the RA. By adjusting the vertical speed of the aircraft, the pilot will endeavour to match the climb rate within the green arc.

Because of the factors mentioned earlier, it is possible that the TCAS software will offer advice which conflicts with an instruction issued by the controller and it is therefore extremely important that pilots are fully aware of the correct procedure to adopt in situations where split-second decisions are needed. This also means that training procedures must be universally co-ordinated across international aviation authorities.

History of the Flights

The Tu-154M, callsign BTC2937, operated by Bashkirian Airlines and registered in Russia, was on a flight from Moscow to Barcelona with 60 passengers, four flight attendants in the cabin and five crew on the flightdeck. The crew consisted of the pilot in command (1), an instructor, who was in the right-hand seat and handling the radio communications and pilot flying the aircraft (2), in the left-hand seat. Behind the pilots were a navigator (3), an engineer (4) and another pilot (5), who was not involved in flying the plane.

The flight had been planned to route via NEGRA, Trasadingen (TRA) VOR and BENOT, entering Zürich airspace at Flight Level 360. After passing Trasadingen, the flight was to be descended to Flight Level 350.

The Tu-154M was cleared by Vienna Radar to fly direct to Trasadingen at FL360. At 21.16 it entered German airspace under the control of Munich Radar, after which it entered Swiss airspace under the control of Zürich Radar at 21.29. The pilot contacted Zürich on 128.05 at 21.30.11.

The Boeing 757-200, callsign DHX611, operated by DHL and registered in Bahrain, was on a trip from Bahrain to Brussels, via Bergamo (Italy). Two pilots were on board. The flight was planned to route via ABESI, KUDES and LOKTA, entering Zürich airspace at FL260, with a request to climb to FL360. The pilot checked in with Zürich Radar on 128.05 at 21.21.

Shortly after the two aircraft had established contact with Zürich Radar, a third flight, an Airbus A320 from Heraklion, Greece, bound for Friedrichshafen airport, checked in with Zürich Radar on frequency 119.925.

Zürich Radar

The control room at Zürich was staffed by two air traffic control officers (ATCOs) and two assistants. It had become normal practice for one ATCO and one assistant to leave the control room at night, when traffic was light. The management at the centre had known about, and tolerated, this practice for some time, even though the duty schedule required two controllers to be on duty at all times. This is what happened on the night of 1 July, with one ATCO leaving the control room at 21.15, and one assistant leaving at 21.25, the remaining ATCO being left to handle all traffic in the sector.

However, on this particular night, work to reorganise the design of the sectors was being carried out by engineering staff. This resulted in the optical short-term conflict alert (STCA) being disabled, and also caused the direct telephone lines to be unavailable between 21.23 and 21.34.

This meant that warnings of a potential loss of separation between aircraft would not be visible on the radar screens, although an aural system was still operative. Also, the telephone links with adjacent control centres were out of action for 11 minutes.

Written directives about the work were available, but they did not include the effect of the work on the ATC equipment. The controllers should have read these directives, but this had not taken place. Instead, they had been verbally briefed about the work.

Three radar screens were available to cover the airspace. One was being used to observe the en-route traffic, and one covered the sector which included the approach to Friedrichshafen airport. When

Diagram showing the tracks of the Boeing 757 and the Tupolev Tu-154M immediately prior to the collision over Überlingen.

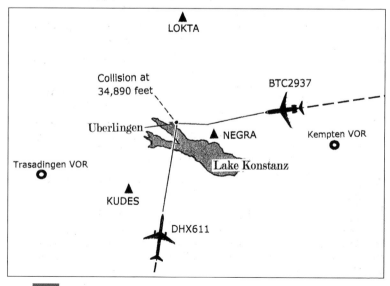

the delayed Airbus came under the control of Zürich Radar, the controller attempted to contact the airport to negotiate the handover. He tried, unsuccessfully, on seven separate occasions, using the telephone bypass system.

In order to deal with the traffic, he had to move between the two radar screens, using two radio frequencies. The problems with the telephone system meant that an excessive amount of time was spent attempting to contact Friedrichshafen, diverting his attention from the 757 and the Tu-154M.

Subsequently, it was discovered that the aural STCA had issued a warning, but this was not heard by the controller or his assistant, possibly because the controller was involved with the Airbus problem.

On Board the Aircraft
Timeline on the Tu-154M
The crew of the Tu-154M were aware of the presence of another aircraft which had appeared on their TCAS screen, and they discussed between themselves the possibility of a conflict developing.

At 21.34.42 the TCAS issued the first Traffic Advisory alert 'Traffic, traffic'. Seven seconds later, at 21.34.49 the controller instructed the crew *'BTC 2937, descend FL350, expedite, I have crossing traffic'*. Obviously, the controller had realised the potential loss of separation and considered that his action would resolve the situation. However, the crew of the Tu-154M did not acknowledge this message, although the pilot in command instructed the pilot flying (PF) to descend.

The control column was pushed forward at 21.34.56, but at the same time the TCAS issued a Resolution Advisory 'Climb, climb'.

At 21.34.59 the pilot flying is heard to say: *'It says climb'*, but the pilot in command says: *'He is guiding us down'*. Four seconds later, the controller repeats his earlier instruction *'BTC 2937, descend FL350, expedite descent, we have traffic at FL360'*.

The pilot in command acknowledged this message: at the same time the navigator called out: *'It's going to pass beneath us'*.

21.35.05 — the control column is pushed fully forward, increasing the rate of descent to 2,000ft per minute.

21.35.24 — the TCAS issues another Resolution Advisory: 'Increase climb, increase climb'.

21.35.27 — the control column is pulled back.

21.35.32 — time of impact.

Timeline on the B757
On the B757, after checking in with Zürich Radar, the pilot requested climb to FL360. This was approved by the controller at 21.25, and the new level was reached at 21.30.

At 21.34.30, the co-pilot left the flightdeck to use the toilet.

21.34.42 — TCAS issues the first Traffic Advisory: 'Traffic, traffic'.

21.34.56 — TCAS issues a Resolution Advisory: 'Descend, descend'.

21.34.58 — the control column is pushed forward.

21.35.12 — TCAS issues a message: 'Increase descent, increase descent'.

21.35.19 — the pilot informs ATC of the descent following the Resolution Advisory. (Apparently, the controller did not hear this message.)

21.35.30 — the control column is pushed fully forward.

21.35.32 — time of impact.

The two aircraft collided at right angles at 34,980ft. The 757 was on a heading of 004°, and the Tu-154M was on a heading of 274°.

The Inquiry

The accident was investigated by the Bundesstelle fur Flugunfalluntersuchung (BFU) (the German Federal Bureau of Aircraft Accidents Investigation), with representatives from Bahrain, the Russian Federation, Switzerland and the United States.

It followed the ICAO approach to the investigation of air accidents, covering the Strategic Level (the background, possibly years or months before the accident), the Tactical Level (when the controller takes charge of the aircraft, some 10 minutes before impact) and the Collision Avoidance Level (when collision avoidance systems, such as Short Term Conflict Alert and TCAS, take over). Incredibly, in this case, all these safety layers failed.

The findings, as would be expected, were thorough, detailed and complex, and only a brief summary is included here. The basic causes were considered to be:

■ the failure of the Zürich ATC system to realise the impending loss of separation between the two aircraft in time to avoid a collision; and

■ The decision of the Russian pilots to follow the controller's instruction to descend, even though this was contrary to the TCAS Resolution Advisory to climb.

However, as in most cases involving aviation and air traffic control related incidents, there are more complex and underlying issues that provide part of the background leading up to the tragedy. In this situation, what has been described as 'a systemic drift into failure' has been identified as a major contributory cause.

The BFU examined several systemic causes, which together combined to create a fatal situation:

■ the regulations and operating procedures of various national aviation authorities, aircraft operators and the TCAS manufacturers were not standardised, were incomplete and were partly contradictory;

■ the management of the Swiss air navigation service company did not ensure that all operating workstations were continuously staffed by air traffic controllers;

■ the practice of having only one controller on duty at night was known to, and tolerated by, the management.

A major part of the investigation concentrated on the procedures to be followed by pilots when faced with conflicting instructions from the TCAS system and ATC, since this was a major contributory cause of the collision.

It was concluded that the wording of the operations manuals covering the use of TCAS by the Tu-154M crew was such that air traffic control instructions had priority over Resolution Advisories issued by the TCAS system.

This is generally in conflict with other guidance published by ICAO, and the TCAS manufacturers, but the investigators still found a degree of confusion within the wording of certain documents.

A series of safety recommendations were made by the BFU, including the following:

■ ICAO should ensure that rules and procedures regarding ACAS are uniform, clear and unambiguous.

■ The procedures for pilots should include the following elements:

■ respond immediately and manoeuvre as indicated, unless doing so would jeopardise the safety of the aeroplane; and never manoeuvre in the opposite sense to an RA.

■ The Russian Federal Aviation Administration should ensure that the TCAS manufacturer rephrases the operating manuals to reflect the regulations and operating procedures in an unambiguous and consistent manner.

One week after the crash, the Director General of EUROCONTROL, Victor Aguado, announced a review and reform of any aspect of air safety which might have played a role in the chain of events leading to the collision.

In August 2002, EUROCONTROL issued a safety bulletin explaining that RAs should be followed at all times. Even sighting another aircraft visually does not provide information on its intentions, and in any case it might not be the one triggering the RA.

Similar bulletins were issued by the UK National Air Traffic Services, pointing out that RAs may be disregarded only when pilots visually identify the conflicting traffic and decide that no deviation from the current flight path is needed. In any case, where an RA and a control instruction are in conflict, the RA should be followed.

ICAO also urged national operators to highlight the critical importance of not manoeuvring in the opposite direction to RA advice.

A high-level Action Group for ATM Safety (AGAS) was set up by EUROCONTROL to examine the safety issues surrounding the Überlingen accident, and one of its recommendations was the investigation of the technical and operational feasibility of downlinking RA information from the flightdeck to the controller's radar screen. As a result, EUROCONTROL set up FARADS — the Feasibility of ACAS RA Downlink Study.

Controllers are made aware of the existence of a Resolution Advisory only if the pilot informs them over the radio; therefore valuable information may be delayed if the pilot is too busy dealing with the situation or if the radio channels are busy. The controller may not be aware that a pilot is departing from an ATC clearance.

There is no doubt that downlinking the information is technically possible (other parameters such as flight levels etc are already being transmitted to the ground) but FARADS aims to examine the wider implications.

These are:
- Evaluation of different technologies, comparing failure modes, delay times and costs;
- Safety studies;
- Evaluating different procedural options;
- Different display options and their human factors assessments.

It now seems probable that Resolution Advisories will eventually be transmitted automatically to controllers, ensuring that they are made aware of a potentially risk-bearing situation shortly after the pilots, helping to prevent the issue of opposite-sense ATC instructions.

Summary

This case highlighted the ongoing need for safety nets to be constantly reviewed, and the ease with which system errors can have dramatic consequences. The loss of separation occurred in good visibility, with very few aircraft in the sector, and should have been easily preventable.

Unfortunately, visualising every gap in complex situations is extremely difficult, even for the experts. Wherever human input is involved, the possibility of failure cannot be ruled out. Often, it is only with hindsight that vulnerable areas can be spotted.

Even though air transport is already an incredibly safe form of transport, the authorities know that no effort should be spared to ensure that it remains so.

4. Airport Procedures

Introduction

European airports are likely to be the limiting factor in air traffic growth over the next 25 years, unless dramatic increases in capacity can be achieved.

Even with an anticipated 60% increase in airport capacity by 2025, EUROCONTROL predicts that the system will be unable to handle 3.5 million flights each year.

The study showed that of the 133 top European airports, three-quarters of them do not expect to be able to add extra runways during the next 20 years.

In 2003, the UK Government published its Air Transport White Paper on airport capacity, proposing that additional runways be provided at Stansted, Heathrow, Luton, Birmingham and Edinburgh, while runway extensions and more terminal capacity are planned for many regional airports.

From the safety aspect, runway incursions continue to be a major hazard, with several serious events occurring, some leading to fatalities.

Airports and Airfields

Airfields vary tremendously in their traffic volume and the type of flights handled. Large commercial airports, such as Heathrow, Gatwick and Manchester, require complex and strict operating systems, combined with an appropriate air traffic structure to cope safely with the traffic.

At the other end of the scale, small landing strips exist for light aircraft and gliders, many with no air traffic control arrangements at all.

The level of protection therefore relates directly to the purpose and type of traffic. Heathrow, for example, is wholly within Class A airspace, offering the highest level of protection, while smaller, less complex locations may be surrounded by an area of Class D airspace which permits all types of flight to access the airfield.

The complexity of airport operations is directly related to the type and volume of traffic handled and although in all cases the basic procedures remain the same, a small provincial airfield dealing only with light aircraft would not be expected to possess the sophisticated aids and facilities of a large-scale operation. Similarly, the number of personnel necessary to provide effective control also increases in proportion to the number of flights.

Control Zones and Control Areas

Around many provincial airfields there will be an area of protected airspace where special air traffic control requirements apply. Details for each airfield are published in the *Aeronautical Information Publication* and the appropriate charts can be obtained from the Civil Aviation Authority, or printed directly from the internet.

The usual arrangement for such airspace at civil airfields consists of Aerodrome Traffic Zones (ATZ), Control Zones (CTR) and Control Areas (CTA).

The Aerodrome Traffic Zone is a circle of controlled airspace, 5 nautical miles in diameter, extending from the surface up to 2,500ft.

The Control Zone extends from ground level (referred to as the surface) up to a specified upper limit — for example, Flight Level 65 (approximately 6,500ft). The zone is cylindrical in shape, centred on the airfield, and is typically 10 nautical miles in diameter. Its purpose is to prohibit any traffic infringing the airspace unless authorised by controllers at the airfield.

At the same time, a further area of regulated airspace extends beyond the zone, and this is known as the Control Area. The upper limit is the same as the zone (FL65 in this example) but the lower limit is perhaps 1,500ft altitude (ie above sea level). The Control Area may be oval in shape, around 20 nautical miles at its longest point, 10 nautical miles across at its narrowest (the same as the zone). The longest axis of the oval shape coincides with the airfield runway headings and therefore provides a protected region of airspace to landing and departing aircraft.

At military airfields, a similar system is used, with an extended portion of airspace on the runway heading, known as a stub.

Flights may, of course, route alongside the zone, and below the Control Area, without infringing regulated airspace, and without necessarily talking to the airfield controller.

Most airfields provide a service to traffic passing through their general area in addition, of course, to those flights wishing to actually land at the airport. Some airfields are included in the Lower Airspace Radar Service (LARS) but even those that are not are still able to offer assistance and advice if conditions and workload permit.

The level of service offered by individual airfields will vary from time to time according to the controllers' workload, the distance of the aircraft from the airfield and the kind of service requested by the pilot, based on the flight conditions under which the aircraft is operating.

Close-up of Qatar Airways A330.
Qatar Airways

If an aircraft is some distance from the airfield radar, and especially if the flight is at low level, the detection on radar will be intermittent and unreliable and the service offered will consequently be reduced.

Advisory Services and Information Services (which are explained in more detail in Chapter 1) are both limited to the extent that not all aircraft in the area are necessarily talking to the controller; pilots cannot be relied upon to remain on a particular track or level since there is no obligation to do so.

Except when under radar control, when a pilot makes contact with the airfield approach (or radar) controller, he/she will identify the flight by callsign, type, level and proposed route and will also request a particular service.

The controller will, after due consideration, inform the pilot of the kind of service being offered, which may be limited by some or all of the factors mentioned earlier.

Many of the aircraft using, or flying in the vicinity of, a local airfield will be under Visual Flight Rules. Their pilots are often unqualified to fly under Instrument Flight Rules; therefore controllers will be unable to instruct pilots to make turns or changes of level which might take them into cloud. At many of the smaller airports, controllers have to handle a mix of large passenger jets and small light aircraft. Where the airport is within Class A airspace, visual flight is not permitted, except that in some cases special traffic lanes are available where certain flights are permitted to fly under Special VFR.

Visual Reference Points

At selected locations around most airfields a number of Visual Reference Points (VRPs) exist for the guidance of pilots operating under Visual Flight Rules. The VRPs are selected from prominent features which can be easily identified from the air — for example, lakes, reservoirs, motorway intersections, power stations, television masts, and so on. Each VRP is also located by reference to its bearing and distance from a radio navigation beacon in the vicinity so that suitably equipped aircraft can cross-check their position.

Pilots operating on VFR will usually be required to route via one of the Visual Reference Points, and, if necessary, to hold at that position while awaiting further clearance.

Use of Transponders

Many flights in contact with local air traffic control will be provided with a transponder, enabling the pilot to transmit the appropriate squawk code.

Most civil and military airfields have an allocation of a small number of squawk codes specifically for their use, which are used by ATC to positively identify aircraft in their region. The transponder codes have no particular meaning; they are allocated at random to flights in the area so that the aircraft position can be detected by secondary radar and indicated on the radar controller's screen. A controller is therefore able to tell which particular air traffic units are handling the flights that are seen on the screen.

In areas of unregulated airspace transponding aircraft will be squawking 7000, the nationally recognised conspicuity code which basically tells the controller that the flight is not receiving a service from ATC.

The use of a transponder is mandatory in the Scottish FIR above 6,000ft and in the London FIR above Flight Level 100. On the other hand, it is not even mandatory for an aircraft to be fitted with a radio (unless it is a Public Transport Flight) when outside controlled airspace.

Airfields

A number of terms can be heard in transmissions concerning manoeuvres near airfields, particularly small airfields where the traffic consists mainly of light aircraft. These terms are best explained by means of an illustration (see diagram) .

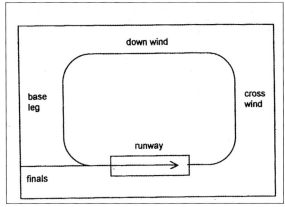

A 'left-hand' circuit is shown, where all turns are to the left; a 'right-hand' pattern would be one where turns are to the right. It is normal practice to operate a left-hand circuit unless air traffic control instructs otherwise. In fact, left-hand circuits will not be referred to by ATC, whereas a right-hand circuit must be specified.

The Visual Circuit

Around each airfield a pattern exists which all flights must follow, unless directed otherwise by ATC. Non-radio traffic also fly under the same pattern, known as the visual circuit. At most airfields, the pattern usually involves turns to the left.

A pilot wishing to approach the landing runway may be permitted to fly along the runway heading on a long final approach. On a straight-in approach a 'Long Final' report is made at between 8nm and 4nm.

Flights which are unable to carry out a straight-in approach will be instructed to enter the circuit by flying 'downwind' — that is, in the opposite direction, and parallel to, the landing runway and some distance to one side. When the aircraft has passed alongside the end of the runway, it will be turned left onto the 'base leg' which is at right angles to the runway heading. As the aircraft reaches the extended centreline of the runway it is turned left again onto the

Final Approach, in line with the runway, in preparation for landing.

Training flights often operate from the smaller airfields, and 'flying the circuit' is common for this purpose. Many flights will not actually land and stop; they will in fact touch down on the runway, continue for a short distance, then take-off and turn left into the circuit pattern for another practice flight. This exercise is referred to as a 'touch and go' circuit.

After departure from the airfield at a specified level, training flights will turn left into the circuit pattern, unless otherwise instructed. This part of the circuit, at right angles to the runway, is known as the 'crosswind' leg and is opposite to the base leg.

At the principal airports, however, local rules and procedures exist which pilots must follow.

Procedural Flights

At airfields where there is no radar, or where an existing radar unit is unserviceable, aircraft are required to make an approach either by visual reference to the field or, in poor weather, to determine the position of the landing runway by making a procedural approach. 'Flying the Procedure' involves positioning the aircraft over a low-powered Non-Directional Beacon (NDB) which may also

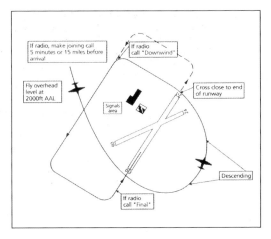

Typical airfield circuit pattern. *CAA*

If radio, make joining call 5 minutes or 15 miles before arrival

If radio call "Downwind"

Fly overhead level at 2000ft AAL

Cross close to end of runway

Signals area

Descending

If radio call "Final"

be referred to as a Locator. This radio facility is usually positioned close to the runway.

Under a procedural approach the aircraft is flown to a position overhead the beacon at a specified level, perhaps 2,500ft. When at the beacon, the aircraft is turned onto a specified heading which takes it away from the airfield, at an angle of 45° to the runway heading. After flying on this heading for one minute, a 180° turn is made to bring the aircraft onto a reciprocal track; a 45° turn is then made to position the aircraft in line with the landing runway.

From this position the pilot commences the descent on the runway centreline and will continue to descend until the airfield decision height is reached. If the runway is not then visible to the pilot, the aircraft must be flown along the runway centreline in the 'Missed Approach Procedure'. The aircraft will be required to continue on the runway heading to a specified level, at which point a turn is made back to the beacon for another attempt.

This kind of exercise is often practised at airfields around the country, both by military and civilian pilots, while undergoing training.

Departures and Arrivals

Routes to and from airports are designed to maximise safety and economy. Charts for individual airports provide details of such routes, usually with separate charts for arrivals and departures.

Routes for departures and arrivals at the major airports are usually detailed as SIDs (Standard Instrument Departures) or STARs (Standard Arrival Routes). In all cases the routeing will be related to radio navigation beacons in the vicinity of the airport and pilots need to position the aircraft using the radial and distance for each particular turning point of the standard route and the points at which particular altitudes need to be achieved. However, the increasing use and reliability of flight management systems are such that the reference to ground-based aids is reducing.

Trials are continuing with a system that allows aircraft with specified flight management systems to fly on Standard Instrument Departure Routes by reference to waypoints which are identified by latitude and longitude co-ordinates only. SIDs which are designed to be flown by aircraft with an approved FMS (flight management system) have been on trial in the UK for several years.

At London Heathrow, a similar trial for fully automatic Standard Arrivals commenced in 2003. This Precision Area Navigation Approach Procedure, involving a small number of aircraft, follows an arrival route, via the Lambourne holding position, to a point eight miles from touchdown on the final approach to each of the airport's runways.

The computers on the flightdeck enable the aircraft to follow a predetermined series of waypoints which are themselves loaded into the database on the aircraft. Under this procedure the crews are not required to cross-check the position of the flight by any other separate method, but, of course, the accuracy and reliability of the process and the equipment have to meet stringent requirements before approval can be given by the aviation authorities.

At airports without instrument approach or departure routes, the aircraft will normally be directed by ATC to the airport radio navigation beacon by means of headings (known as 'vectoring') until approach control takes over and routes the flight onto the extended centreline of the landing runway.

Departures

Before departure, all passenger or freight-carrying aircraft which are expecting to enter controlled airspace are required to file a flight plan detailing various aspects of the proposed flight. Flight plans are prepared by the individual airlines and sent electronically to the Central Flow Management Unit (CFMU) of EUROCONTROL, at one of two processing centres in Haren and Bretigny.

Plans may be submitted many months before the day of the flight, since many scheduled services will be known well in advance. At the CFMU the details are automatically checked for errors. For example, planning to fly south on a route which is designated for northbound traffic would result in the plan being rejected.

Standard Arrival Routes into Edinburgh, via TWEED. Civil Aviation Authority

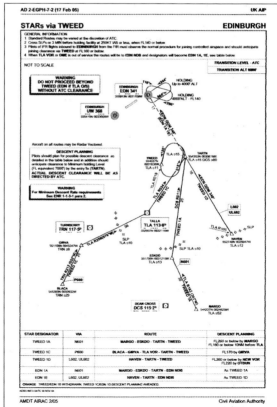

The plans are handled through three phases: Strategic, covering a period of several months to a couple of days before the flight, when overall traffic predictions are prepared; followed by the Pre-Tactical level, covering the two days before the flight, where action is taken to fine tune the air traffic system; and finally the Tactical level, on the day of the flight, where air traffic flow management adjustments are made.

When the clearance is issued by the CFMU, it may include a departure slot time which is based on the aircraft's Calculated Take-off Time (CTOT). The slot will have been derived from the flight plan and will ensure a smooth passage through the various areas of responsibility that the aircraft will pass. It is important that the departure controller and the aircraft operator recognise the importance of complying with slot times so as to prevent bottlenecks in the system and controller overload. The slot time allows for the flight to depart with a tolerance of minus 5 minutes or plus 10 minutes to allow for local conditions. Where it is not possible to meet this requirement a new flight plan has to be filed with the CFMU. Various capacity improvements in the last few years have resulted in a significant reduction in delays due to ATC factors, even though traffic has increased year on year. In fact, the average delay to flights in UK airspace, caused by air traffic management issues, is now less than 30 seconds, compared to several minutes a few years ago.

Daily replanning of the major routes through European airspace, thus avoiding bottlenecks and overloading of busy sectors, means that delays on the ground due to the ATC system have been significantly reduced.

At present, all UK airports, except Stansted, use a system of paper strips to identify individual flights. They are also

Trial Precision Navigation Approach procedure for Runway 26 Left at Gatwick.
Civil Aviation Authority

TRIAL P-RNAV INITIAL APPROACH PROCEDURE   LONDON GATWICK
to RWY 26L ILS Final Approach (Day)

GENERAL INFORMATION
1 Trial Procedure available to approved participating aircraft with RNAV systems functionality equal to or better than that specified in JAA TGL-10 for P-RNAV operations in terminal airspace.
2 Procedures incorporate continuous descent approach profile. Approximate distances to touchdown shown in brackets.
3 Procedures reflect daytime (0600-2330HRS local) noise abatement requirements for joining Final Approach.
4 Participating aircraft will be cleared initially via appropriate conventional STAR prior to clearance for RNAV Initial Approach.
5 Loss of Communications Procedure: If clearance has been given and acknowledged, continue with Trial P-RNAV procedure to join ILS if able, otherwise adopt the Standard (Conventional) Loss of Communications Procedure for London Gatwick via appropriate conventional STAR.
6 All waypoints are fly-by.

TRANSITION ALT   6000
MAG VAR   2.5°W

MSA 25NM

used to record details of any instructions issued by the controller, together with the pilot's responses. These are known as Flight Progress Strips (FPS), and they contain the complete 'history' of the traffic being handled by an airport or air traffic control centre.

The strips, which are automatically generated by the system some 15 minutes ahead, are arranged in front of the controller in the order in which they will be actioned, colour coded as departures or arrivals. Blue strips indicate departures, brown strips indicate arrivals. As the controller issues an instruction, the detail is entered by hand on the strip.

Stansted switched over to electronic strips late in 2004, the first UK airport to abandon the paper method. Many countries now operate this system, and paper strips will eventually disappear. One significant advantage is the ability to share information electronically with other controllers, something which is not possible with paper strips and handwritten notes.

Arrivals
With the exception of small local airfields, aircraft arriving at an airport are first transferred to the airport approach frequency by the ATCC. Airport information may be obtained from recorded messages or directly from the ATC personnel. Aircraft are 'vectored' to a position that places them in line with the landing runway, after which the aircraft will lock on to the ILS radio transmissions. If ILS is not available, a visual approach may be possible, or alternatively a surveillance radar approach will be provided by approach control.

Flights will have been cleared to a local reporting point, usually an NDB, following which approach control will direct the pilot to a position which will enable an approach to the landing runway.

Pilots who are not qualified to fly on instruments will be unable to use this method but will alternatively operate under a visual system.

An alternative method used more and more frequently is 'self positioning' or 'centrefix', where the aircraft is positioned on the extended centreline of the runway using the aircraft's on-board navigation system.

Runways
The runways at an airport are designated according to their compass bearings, rounded off to the nearest 10°, with the final zero omitted. For example, a runway which faces almost due west (say 266°) would be rounded up to 270° and described as 'Runway 27'. The same runway, used in the opposite direction, will be facing due east and will differ by 180° to be 086°. It will then be rounded up to 'Runway 09'. Where two parallel runways are available, as at Heathrow, they are known as 'left' and 'right' respectively. Occasionally, knowledge of individual runways is helpful to airband listeners, especially where only the aircraft radio transmissions can be heard, since one of the clues to the destination may be the 'runway in use' quoted by the controller. Hearing the words 'Cleared DAYNE One Alpha Arrival for 24 left' identifies the destination as Manchester because DAYNE is a reporting point on the Standard Arrival Route.

The ILS consists of two radio transmissions: the 'localizer', which indicates the centreline of the runway, and the 'glide path', a horizontal beam angled upwards at 3° to provide the correct angle of approach.

Holding
During busy periods, arriving aircraft may be required to delay their approach because of weather or traffic congestion, and this is known as holding. Where delays are expected, flights may be held at high level many miles from the airport until they are able to descend and join the airfield holding pattern.

Various holding patterns are available near main airports, and aircraft fly a

Turkish Airlines Airbus A310. Author

racetrack pattern until an approach is possible, or alternatively a decision to divert is made. Standard holding patterns may themselves become congested and in such cases aircraft may be required to hold by flying between navigation beacons, many miles from the airport.

Holding patterns near airports are sometimes referred to as stacks because aircraft are stacked one above the other with 1,000ft separation. As the flight at the lowest level is cleared to leave the hold, other flights descend in 1,000ft steps. Flights which are required to hold will be requested, for example, to 'Enter the hold at Lambourne FL90'. Full details of holding patterns are given on arrival charts for individual airfields. If a short delay is expected the controller will inform the pilot that the delay is less than 20 minutes. If the delay is longer pilots will be given an indication of the length of time they can be expected to hold and they will also be given an Expected Approach Time (EAT), which is the time the flight can expect to leave the lowest level of the holding stack to commence an approach to the destination airfield.

Occasionally, if one of the stacks is particularly congested, a flight may be re-routed to an alternative holding point so that the delay may be kept to a minimum. Arriving flights are monitored by the traffic manager at the control centre and are allocated arrival sequence numbers generated by computer, to provide the most efficient arrival pattern.

Categories 1, 2 and 3

Airports provided with an Instrument Landing System (ILS) conform with one of three categories enabling suitably equipped aircraft to land in varying degrees of poor visibility.

Airfields have various categories for approaching flights allocated to the different runways and basically these are in accordance with the following rules:

Category I (Cat I) Operation

A precision instrument approach and landing with a decision height not lower than 200ft and with either a visibility not less than 800 metres or a runway visual range of not less than 550 metres.

Category II (Cat II) Operation

A precision instrument approach and landing with a decision height lower than 200ft but not lower than 100ft, and a runway visual range not less than 350 metres.

Category IIIA (Cat IIIA) Operation

A precision instrument approach and

landing with either a decision height lower than 100ft or with no decision height, and a runway visual range not less than 200 metres.

Category IIIB (Cat IIIB) Operation

A precision instrument approach and landing with either a decision height lower than 50ft or with no decision height, and a runway visual range less than 200 metres but not less than 50 metres.

Category IIIC (Cat IIIC) Operation

A precision instrument approach and landing with no decision height and no runway visual range limitations.

During Cat II and Cat III operations, special Low Visibility Procedures have to be implemented to ensure that there is no adverse effect on the instrument landing system signals. Usually this means that the holding positions for departing aircraft are further back from the runway than otherwise and also aircraft clearing the runway need to be at greater distances before reporting that they have vacated. Special lighting and marker boards are positioned at the holding points and at runway exits to indicate the limits of the sensitive areas.

Approach Monitoring

At Heathrow and Gatwick airports approaches to the landing runways are assisted by the use of an Approach Monitoring Aid (AMA). This consists of a special radar in the Visual Control Room which shows a zone which projects along the runway centreline for 5 or 6 miles in a funnel-shaped area which indicates to the controller the position of approaching aircraft. Where a particular aircraft is seen to stray from the protected area the system automatically alerts the controller by indicating the aircraft callsign and the runway which it was approaching. The screen indicates the previous eight recorded radar indications so that the controller can see the deviation from the required centreline track. Depending on the distance from touchdown the controller will instruct the pilot to carry out a missed approach or, alternatively, advise the pilot

so that the aircraft can be steered onto the correct centreline.

Microwave Landing Systems

The current Instrument Landing Systems (ILSs) in use at virtually all airports are becoming inadequate for the increasing volume of aircraft, and in addition changes in regulations regarding radio frequencies means that ILS is becoming less reliable.

The replacement system being suggested is the Microwave Landing System (MLS), which operates on frequencies around 5GHz which are virtually free from interference. The system also has the advantage of allowing aircraft to lock on to the final approach anywhere within a 25-mile segment — in other words, aircraft can fly a curved approach instead of a straight-line approach as with ILS.

However, MLS is expensive for airlines and airports and alternative systems are being examined. Tests are ongoing for a satellite navigation aid to bring aircraft onto the final approach. Any adjustments to the aircraft's position are made by a ground-based station which corrects the Global Position System information so that the aircraft is in the exact position for landing. The system is known as the Differential Global Positioning System (DGPS).

The advantage for airlines lies in the fact that many of their aircraft are already fitted with GPS equipment so it makes sense to use it for landings.

In 2004, London Heathrow became the first airport in the world to introduce MLS.

Autonomous Precision Approach and Landing System (APALS)

A further replacement for traditional airport landing systems depends on the use of global positioning to arrive in the vicinity of an airfield, at which point the existing weather radar fitted on the flightdeck is used to compare the photographic images stored in a databank for the particular airfield with the radar view of the terrain ahead of the aircraft. The computer system adjusts the flight continuously in an effort to match the ground details with the stored images until the two coincide exactly.

Aerodrome Traffic Monitoring

Monitoring of traffic at some airports is now in use. The benefits of Aerodrome Traffic Monitoring (ATM) are the improved methods for determining the landing order spacing and distance from touchdown of individual flights. The controller is able to provide information on various flights to other pilots, to assist with appropriate separation for departing aircraft and confirmation that a departing flight is following its correct track in accordance with the ATC clearance. It is also possible for the equipment to confirm correct squawk codes, ensure appropriate separation between aircraft, monitor flights accurately in the event of a missed approach and to decide on the most appropriate action to be taken where separation between aircraft is lost.

High-Intensity Runway Operations

Heathrow uses its runways to maximum efficiency by a number of special operating procedures. For example, an aircraft on final approach may be given clearance to land if the preceding aircraft is still on the runway but is at least 2,500 metres from the threshold when the landing aircraft crosses the threshold. This means that while aircraft are clearing the runway at the furthest exits the next aircraft can be given clearance to land.

Obviously, the shorter the time an aircraft actually occupies the runway the more landings can be accommodated. Pilots need to organise their landing procedures to achieve a minimum occupancy time so that the maximum landing rates can be maintained. The proposed exit should be identified, together with the correct rate of deceleration, so that the aircraft leaves the runway with the minimum of delay.

Research at Heathrow has shown that significant improvements to Runway Occupancy Times (ROTs) can be made by more efficient planning of exit procedures. Similarly, departing aircraft ROTs can be improved if the aircraft is able to take-off without delay. Again, research has shown that when an aircraft is holding on the runway awaiting departure clearance, there can be a delay in reacting to the controller's instruction to take-off of 11 seconds. In many instances delays of 15 to 30 seconds occur. A reduction in these delays would permit an extra two departures per hour.

Procedures to reduce ROTs are being introduced at airports across Europe with

The Heathrow Final Approach Spacing Tool (FAST) is a computer-based method for assisting controllers in achieving arrival rates with greater accuracy and consistency by indicating when to initiate turns. NATS

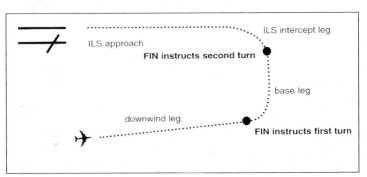

High Intensity Runway Operations (HIRO). Airlines need to decide on accurate and realistic occupancy times for the runways at each airport to be specified and supplied to the controlling authorities to enable them to optimise their approach procedures.

Late in 2000, the Air Traffic Management Development Centre commenced operational trials of the Final Approach Spacing Tool (FAST) to test the accuracy and consistency of the spacing of aircraft on final approach so that the ATC workload, particularly that of the final director, would be decreased. The concept calculates accurately the times and positions for aircraft turning onto base leg and final approach.

Automatic Terminal Information Service (ATIS)

Details of weather conditions and airport information is described in detail in the chapter on weather information.

At small airfields information about weather conditions is transmitted directly by the control personnel, FISOs or Air/Ground radio operators, but at larger airports such details are often provided by pre-recorded tapes broadcast on a continuous basis. Many airports now have an information service that is broadcast on a dedicated frequency (the ATIS). The information is identified by letter, changing at regular intervals, and aircraft are requested to indicate the identification letter to approach control on first radio contact.

Below is a transcript of a typical ATIS broadcast:

'Good morning this is Heathrow Information INDIA zero eight one five hours weather. Three two zero degrees, less than five knots. Two thousand two hundred metres. Mist. Scattered at two thousand five hundred feet, broken at five thousand feet. Temperature three, dewpoint three. QNH one zero zero seven millibars. The landing runway is two seven left, departure runway two

seven right. Please confirm your aircraft type and report information INDIA received on first contact with Heathrow.'
When the pilot contacts Approach Control the transmission will include the aircraft type and the identification of the Arrival information. For example:
'Heathrow Approach Speedbird six two five, seven three seven with INDIA, flight level eight zero, eight miles to run to Ockham.'

Datalink Automatic Terminal Information Services (D-ATIS) are now available at Manchester and Gatwick airports. These

The new control tower under construction at London Heathrow airport in March 2005.
Author

provide pilots of suitably equipped aircraft with printouts of the current weather, plus details of any other relevant information — for example, taxiways which are closed.

London Heathrow

The procedures described here are used at Heathrow, but the principles will be very similar at most civil airports.

London Heathrow is a particularly busy and complex airport, handling more international traffic than any other airport in the world. There are two parallel runways designated 27 Left, 27 Right, 09 Left and 09 Right. The headings of the runways are 270° (to the nearest 10°) in one direction and 090° when used in the opposite direction. As there are two parallel runways they are known as 'Left' or 'Right', as viewed by a pilot arriving or departing.

Before 2 July 1987 the two main runways at Heathrow were designated as 28 and 10 but because of small annual changes in the magnetic bearing of the North Pole the runway directions are now closer to 270°/090° than 280°/010°.

A separate, rarely used, runway is 23, which is on a heading of 230°.

In normal operating conditions the '27' runways are used (one for departures, one for arrivals) since they face the prevailing winds. By local agreement, runway 'switching' takes place every day at around 07.00hrs and 15.00hrs (local), thus giving the residents under the flight paths some relief from the almost continuous streams of traffic.

The 09 runways are used when the wind direction is from the east or when major public events are taking place in central London, so as to reduce the likelihood of aircraft flying low over the area.

Heathrow Control Tower

The control tower at Heathrow contains the visual control room (VCR) — the glazed room at the top of the tower. The

Aerodrome chart for London Heathrow.
Civil Aviation Authority

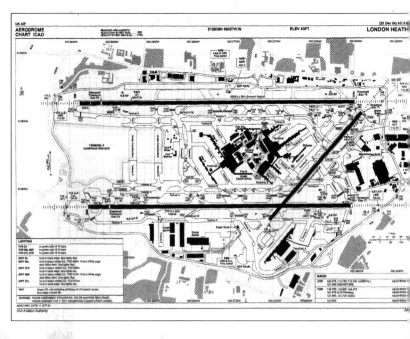

Standard Instrument Departure routes from Heathrow via Midhurst.
Civil Aviation Authority

MIDHURST SIDs

LONDON HEATHROW

GENERAL INFORMATION
1 SIDs reflect Noise Preferential Routeings. See EGLL AD 2.21 for Noise Abatement Procedures.
2 Initial climb straight ahead to 583' QNH (500' GFE).
3 Cross Noise Monitoring Points not below 1057' QNH (1000' GFE) thereafter maintain minimum 4% climb gradient to 4000' (Note climb gradients greater than 4% may be required for ATC and airspace purposes) to comply with Noise Abatement requirements.
4 Callsign for RTF frequency used when established after take off "London Control". Report callsign, SID designator, current altitude and cleared altitude on first contact with "London Control".
5 En-route cruising level will be issued after take-off by "London Control". Do not climb above SID levels until instructed by ATC.
6 Maximum IAS 250KT below FL100 unless otherwise authorised.

NOT TO SCALE

TRANSITION ALT 6000'

(Chart content — Midhurst SID diagram with routeing waypoints: BUR 421, LON 113·9°, MID 114·0°, MIDHURST, LON o5, LON o1·5, LON o3·5, LON s2, LON s5·5, LON o8, LON o12, LON o17, MID o10, MID o15, MID o19, MID o12, MID o8, etc.)

WARNING
Due to interaction with other routes do NOT climb above 6000' until cleared by ATC.

AVERAGE
TRACK MILEAGE
TO MID VOR
MID 4F 31
MID 3G 50
MID 3H 28
MID 3J 29
MID 3K 29

MIDHURST
MID 114·0°
5162'44N 000733'W

SID	RWY	ROUTEING (incl. Noise Preferential Routeing)	ALTITUDES	AIRWAY ROUTE
MID 4F 133·175	27R	Straight ahead to intercept LON VOR R254. At LON o5 turn left onto BUR NDB QDR 164°. At LON o12 turn right onto MID VOR R015 to MID VOR.	Cross LON o8 above 3000'	Via MID A34
MID 3G 133·175	27L	Straight ahead to intercept LON VOR R242 until LON o5·5, then turn left onto BUR NDB QDR 164°. At LON o12 turn right onto MID VOR R015 to MID VOR.	LON o12 above 4000' LON o17 (MID o10) above 5000'	N615(via BOGNA. HARDY to join M605) Southbound
MID 3H 133·175	23	Straight ahead to intercept BUR NDB QDR 164°. At LON o12 turn right onto MID VOR R015 to MID VOR.	MID VOR at 6000'	
MID 3J 133·175	09R	Straight ahead to LON s2, then turn right onto LON VOR R127 until LON o3·5, then turn right onto MID VOR R029 to MID VOR.	Cross LON o19 at 3000' or above (09R 5%) (BSL 4.9%)	
MID 3K 133·175	09L	Straight ahead to LON o1·5, then turn right onto LON VOR R127 until LON o3·5, then turn right onto MID VOR R029 to MID VOR.	MID o15 at 4000' or above MID o12 at 5000' or above MID o8 at 6000'	

CHANGE: LON RADIALS UPDATED.

AERO INFO DATE 1 DEC 03

AMDT 2/04

Civil Aviation Authority

VCR team consists of the Ground Movement Planner and the Ground Movement Controller, and their Assistants. On a raised area in the centre of the room sit the Air Arrivals Controller (AAC) and the Air Departures Controller (ADC). These two controllers sit alongside each other facing the two runways in use — the holding point of the departure runway and the touchdown point of the arrival runway. If the runways in use are reversed, the AAC and the ADC turn to face the opposite direction, facing again the appropriate runways.

The Approach Controllers are located at West Drayton in the Terminal Operations Room, where traffic from all the London airports is handled.

Heathrow Departures

With the volume of traffic involved it would be impossible for every pilot to be given an individual flight clearance over the radio — the airwaves would soon become clogged with controllers and pilots trying to pass messages to each other. In order to relieve airband congestion, the various departures for aircraft leaving busy airports have been classified into specific routes, known as Standard Instrument Departures (or SIDs).

When a pilot initially calls the Ground Movement Planner, he/she will be aware of the SID to be followed and ATC will confirm the clearance. In the first message the pilot will also quote the stand at which the aircraft is parked, and the weather details taken from a recorded ATIS broadcast. The reply from ATC will specify the SID and also the secondary radar identity squawk code.

Aircraft requesting a clearance to start engines will first contact the Ground Movement Planner in the Visual Control Room. This approval will be given, together with details of the ATC clearance, and the pilot will then be handed on to the Ground Movement Controller who will issue permission to 'pushback' from the aircraft stand. Taxi clearance to the holding point of the departure runway will also be given.

As the holding point is approached, the pilot will be asked to monitor the frequency

DOVER SIDs/DETLING SIDs   LONDON HEATHROW

Standard Instrument departure routes from London Heathrow via Dover /Detling.
Civil Aviation Authority

controller to give the SID letter, current level (or passing level) and cleared level. The controller must confirm that these details comply with the initial clearance.

After departure from Heathrow the aircraft will be handed on to the Terminal Control Centre at West Drayton for onward clearance through the London FIR airways system. Note that the words 'take-off' are used exclusively as part of the clearance to actually leave the ground. At all other times the word 'departure' is used.

of the Air Departures Controller, who will give clearance to enter the active runway, line up and eventually take-off.

Each of these operations will be on a different radio frequency.

Soon after the aircraft is airborne the pilot will be instructed to contact the Approach Controller, or, in the case of the London airports, the London TMA controller at West Drayton for onward clearance.

Departing aircraft will follow the appropriate Standard Instrument Departure route. As there have been a significant number of problems associated with aircraft exceeding their initial cleared level it is now a requirement for the pilot on first contact with the departure radar

Heathrow Arrivals

At Heathrow, as at most of the larger airfields, arrivals to the airport are via a series of standardised routes referred to as STARs (Standard Arrival Routes). These are designated by reference to the name of the holding point and a particular letter code, which is changed if there is a variation in the route. Standard Arrival charts are available through recognised chart suppliers.

Aircraft inbound for Heathrow are usually required to route via one of four reporting points: Lambourne and Bovingdon to the north, Ockham and

JMC Airlines Boeing 757. Author

Biggin to the south. If necessary, flights will be required to 'hold' over one of the reporting points, at 1,000ft separation levels, entering the 'stack' at the highest level and gradually stepping down, 1,000ft at a time, until clearance is given to leave the hold at the lowest level for an approach to the airport.

As aircraft approach one of the four reporting points, flights will contact Heathrow Approach. After leaving the stack, the No 1 Radar Directors bring the traffic from the four reporting points into two flows towards the extended centreline of the runway. Control then passes to the No 2 Director who combines the two separate flows into one stream of traffic ready for landing. At 6 nautical miles from touchdown, control is passed to the Air Arrivals Controller who gives the clearance to land. After landing, as the aircraft clears the runway, control is taken over by the Ground Movement Controller, who directs the aircraft to its parking stand.

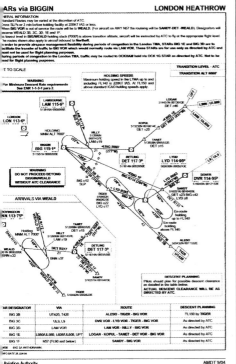

Standard Arrival Routes into Heathrow via Biggin.
Civil Aviation Authority

5. The North Atlantic System

Introduction

Passenger convenience, differences in time zones, and noise limitations at many airports mean that much of the North Atlantic traffic is divided into one of two flows.

The westbound flow leaves the European airports in the morning, crossing the UK and enters the North Atlantic during the late morning and early afternoon, arriving in the US and Canada in the late afternoon European time.

Most of these flights will be 'turned around' in a few hours, returning to Europe as the eastbound flow, touching down in the early morning, ready for the whole process to be repeated.

This results in most of the air traffic being concentrated in a one-way stream with a mid-Atlantic peak of westbound traffic between 11.00 and 19.00 UTC, and a peak of opposite direction eastbound traffic between 02.00 and 07.00 UTC.

The air traffic control responsibility for traffic in the eastern half of the North Atlantic lies with National Air Traffic Services, through the Oceanic Control Centre, based at Prestwick, Scotland. Although this centre controls the traffic, radio communications are handled through a radio station near Shannon, Ireland. The combination of Shannon and Prestwick, was used to create the callsign 'Shanwick'.

Traffic Volume

A large proportion of the commercial flights which route through UK airspace are on transatlantic journeys. As well as those from airports in Britain, many flights will be from all parts of Europe and the Middle East.

Shanwick Oceanic Operations Room.
Shanwick OCC

The number of transatlantic flights dropped significantly following the terrorist attacks in America in 2001, and it was only in 2004 that it returned to the pre-2001 level. It is now continuing to increase at around 5% per year.

At busy times of the year it is now possible for 1,000 flights to cross the North Atlantic in one 24-hour period. Many of these flights will route through UK airspace and they can be heard on a suitable airband radio.

Reduced Vertical Separation Minima

Due to the increasing volume of flights, ultimately leading to congestion on the North Atlantic routes, the aviation authorities spent several years examining the implications of a reduction in the vertical separation between aircraft, from 2,000ft to 1,000ft, as a means of creating additional capacity.

In March 1997 the first stage of the reduced vertical separation minima programme was introduced in the North Atlantic region, changing the separation from 2,000ft to 1,000ft. Initially, two additional flight levels became available: FL340 and FL360. This provided the airlines with more choice when selecting cruising levels, often resulting in considerable economies for each trip.

For aircraft to operate under RVSM, they are required to have the required navigational capability known as MASPS (Minimum Aircraft System Performance Specification). Individual aircraft have to be certified for MASPS capability by their State of Registry.

Later, the additional flight levels 320 and 380 were introduced, leaving only Flight Levels 300 and 400 unavailable. These final two levels were added to the RVSM programme on 19 April 2001, coinciding with the implementation of RVSM in UK and Irish airspace. RVSM was introduced in mainland Europe in 2002.

Close-up of Shanwick Oceanic Operations Room. Shanwick OCC

The RVSM programme meant that an extra six flight levels became available, giving more airlines the scope for selecting the most suitable level, while at the same time more flights could be accommodated.

In the early days of RVSM, flights leaving the North Atlantic and entering domestic airspace were required to change over from the 1,000ft system to the traditional 2,000ft vertical separation. This created some complications for radar control units and retraining for controllers was essential prior to the complete introduction of RVSM.

Height Monitoring

Prior to the introduction of RVSM the accuracy of height keeping had to be assessed before the authorities were confident that the system would operate safely. One height monitoring unit (HMU) was established near Aberporth, in West Wales, on the centreline of airway Upper Golf One (now renamed Upper Lima Nine) with a second at Gander. Airlines wishing to be certified for the reduced levels were required to overfly the HMUs in order that the various special radars in the area could track the exact height of each flight as it passed overhead.

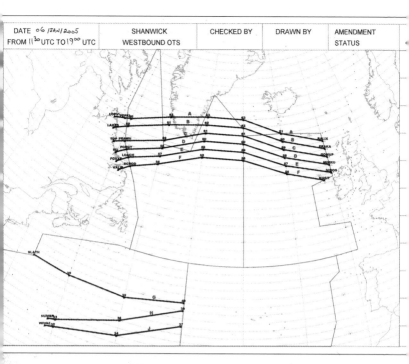

HMUs are now located in Germany and Austria, where they are used for monitoring aircraft levels.

Transition Airspace

Two blocks of upper airspace, between the UK domestic airspace and the North Atlantic, act as transition areas under the command of controllers at Shannon. These enable flights to be co-ordinated efficiently as they approach or leave Shanwick airspace. The southern area is SOTA (the Shannon Oceanic Transition Area), and the recently introduced area to the north is known as NOTA (the Northern Oceanic Transition Area).

Reduced Horizontal Separation

Reduced Horizontal Separation Minima (RHSM) is being considered for operational use on the North Atlantic. This

An example of a northerly system of North Atlantic tracks for 6 January 2005.
Shanwick OCC

means that the present 60-nautical-mile lateral separation will be reduced to 30 nautical miles and the 10-minute time difference between aircraft at the same level will be reduced to 5 minutes. RHSM depends on the successful introduction of improved communication and surveillance systems. Automatic Dependent Surveillance (ADS) provides position reports on the aircraft location which are issued automatically and which update the Flight Data Processing System (FDPS) at Shanwick. Datalink reporting has to be highly reliable and able to cope with 'worst case' situations and emergencies.

North Atlantic Track System

The routes across the Atlantic are known as 'tracks', and they are revised twice every 24 hours, once in each direction. The tracks often vary considerably from day to day, the main consideration being the weather, with particular attention being paid to the high-speed winds known as 'jet streams' which can significantly affect the economy of long flights.

Planners on both sides of the Atlantic, at Gander in Newfoundland and at Prestwick, Scotland, consult over the daily track construction, with Gander being responsible for the night-time tracks, and Prestwick for the day-time tracks.

Eastbound night-time tracks are valid between 22.00 and 08.00 UTC, and westbound day-time tracks are valid between 08.00 and 19.00 UTC. (In both cases the times apply at 30° west.)

Details of the daily track system are passed directly to airlines that regularly use the Atlantic and to airports that are situated close to the oceanic boundary. Prior to 1995, details of the daily track system were broadcast on a dedicated VHF channel between 09.00 and 19.00, but this service no longer exists. Instead, track details are transmitted directly to interested organisations, and they can also be accessed on the Internet.

Charts

The boundary between oceanic airspace and the London, Scottish and Shannon UIRs is shown on charts produced by the various publishers. They also show the whole of the North Atlantic and are therefore useful for tracking flights between Europe and the American continent. The actual entry/exit points to the oceanic control area coincide with whole degrees of latitude and longitude, and these are also depicted on the charts.

It is helpful to plot the track co-ordinates on a globe, the advantage being that a globe can be used to show direct lines between two points on the earth's surface

British Midland Airbus A320. bmi

(known as 'great circle' routes). It is then easy to appreciate, for example, that a straight line between Paris and Los Angeles takes a flight in a northerly direction over Scotland.

Polar Routes

A separate route structure is also available for flights across the North Pole is also available for traffic on the Europe/Alaska axis. Again these tracks are uni-directional through the Reykjavik CTA with a westbound peak between 12.00 and 18.00 UTC and an eastbound peak between 00.01 and 06.00 UTC. For this traffic a Polar Track Structure (PTS), consisting of 10 fixed tracks, is available.

Radio Frequencies

Before a flight is allowed to enter North Atlantic airspace, the crew must obtain an 'oceanic clearance' direct from Shanwick. This is normally done when the aircraft is in flight over the UK.

One difference between 'oceanic' and 'domestic' (the term often used to refer to the control system over land) is that the VHF radio frequencies used to obtain oceanic clearances do not have any relation to the different frequencies used when flying under radar control.

Irrespective of its location, an aircraft requesting oceanic clearance will always use one of two frequencies, 123.95MHz, or 127.65MHz. (A third frequency, 135.52MHz, was also available until it was withdrawn in 2004, since many airlines now obtain their clearances by datalink.)

123.95MHz is used by aircraft registered west of 30° west, while 127.65MHz is used by aircraft registered east of 30° west. In practice, this generally means that American and Canadian airlines use 123.95, and British and European airlines use 127.65.

On the European side of the Atlantic, the clearances for aircraft to follow a particular oceanic track are obtained from the Oceanic Area Control Centre, using the callsign 'Shanwick'.

Several tracks are arranged each day. Usually, there are four to six, offering airlines a reasonable choice for their particular flights. The westbound tracks are identified by the letters 'Alpha', 'Bravo', 'Charlie' and so on, with 'Alpha' being the most northerly. In the past it was possible to have as many as 10 tracks in operation, but with the introduction of reduced vertical separation this is no longer necessary.

Eastbound tracks, between North America and Europe, are allocated a series of letters, commencing with 'Zulu' as the most southerly track, followed by 'Yankee' as the next track to the north, then 'X-ray' and so on.

The daily decisions regarding track positions depend so much on the prevailing weather conditions that wide variations can be seen throughout the year.

MNPS Airspace

The airspace over most of the North Atlantic between 27,500ft and 40,000ft is classified as Class A, and is known as MNPS airspace (Minimum Navigation Performance Specification airspace). Aircraft are required to satisfy certain criteria concerning navigation capabilities. It is obviously very important that aircraft which are out of radar contact must be able to navigate with a very high degree of reliability, especially as the airspace is extremely congested.

Oceanic Clearances

After departure, when the aircraft is at a height which will permit satisfactory radio contact, the aircrew may call 'Shanwick' on one of the frequencies mentioned earlier. The second radio will be used (often referred to as the 'number two box' both by aircrew and ATC). Alternatively, datalinking may be used by suitably equipped aircraft.

Shanwick will have details of the flight and the requested track shown on the flight plan. A typical example of a request for oceanic clearance is given later. Remember that such transmissions can be heard anywhere in the UK — transatlantic

traffic crosses virtually all areas of the country so that radio reception is almost guaranteed.

Clearances from Shanwick are transmitted from remote VHF radio stations at Dundonald Hill (near Prestwick), Davidstow Moor in Cornwall, Mangersta (Outer Hebrides) and Grantham (in Lincolnshire). Sometimes aircrew will mention their point of departure in the transmission, and (more likely) the destination will be quoted. Also, the track letter and the entry point will be given at the beginning of the message, thus giving the listener a strong lead to the location of the flight. For example, a point of entry of SOMAX (50° north and 15° west), being west of Land's End, indicates the position of the flight in the southwest of England in the English Channel area.

Some of the destination points may not be easily understood, simply because aircrew may refer to airports by their local names. For example, oceanic clearances to 'Kennedy' or to 'Mirabelle' are for New York and Montreal respectively. To fully understand all the various names you will need a suitable reference book on airports or a selection of airline timetables.

Some airlines will contact Shanwick on VHF radio to request their oceanic clearance, the busiest period normally being between 11.00 and 15.00. However, around two-thirds of transatlantic flights now obtain clearances via datalink, cutting out the need for voice communication. Eventually, most airlines will use this method, and the only VHF transmissions will be where complications have arisen or where the equipment has failed.

Icelandair Boeing 757-300. Icelandair

It is unlikely that the VHF replies from Shanwick will be received in most parts of the United Kingdom, but as the clearances are often read back in full by the aircrew there should be no problem in understanding the details. The major airlines, however, which regularly cross the North Atlantic, are not usually required to give a full readback.

After the initial clearance is requested, several minutes will pass before Shanwick recalls the flight. The track co-ordinates will then be passed to the aircraft, and details are read back by the aircrew. Some of the requested tracks, however, may not be available, for a variety of reasons, and alternative flight levels, or even a change of track, may be offered. Occasionally the 'bargaining' may continue for some time before an acceptable route is agreed between the pilot and Shanwick.

Track Details

The oceanic clearance will specify the track by its appropriate code letter, the flight level (including any en-route changes) the track co-ordinates, and the cleared Mach number.

Approximately one flight every hour will be asked to send meteorological reports as it progresses on its journey, referred to as 'SEND MET'.

The daily track allocation includes a unique reference number based simply on the actual day of the year, known as the Track Message Identification Number (TMI). For example, on the last day of

January the TMI will be 031. The intention of giving each series of tracks this identification ensures against aircrews inadvertently operating on incorrect data. The TMI will be included in the pilot's acknowledgement; in these cases the full track message does not have to be read back.

Before preparing the flight plan, due consideration is given to the various available tracks, and the final choice is that which provides the most suitable route. It follows, therefore, that regular flights may choose several different tracks throughout the year, depending on the suitability of the various available routes. This means that although a particular flight may regularly cross the UK on a particular airway it is inevitable that now and then a different track will be chosen when conditions are suitable.

For Atlantic crossings, relative speed between aircraft is determined by the Mach number technique, the ratio of the aircraft speed compared to the speed of sound at a particular flight level. (Mach .75 would be three-quarters the speed of sound, for example.) Two aircraft, at the same flight level, experiencing the same conditions of wind speed and temperature are more likely to maintain safe separation if they both use the same Mach number. Part of the oceanic clearance will specify the Mach number to be maintained.

Navigation across the Atlantic is achieved by use of the Inertial Navigation System (INS), of which there are three

North Atlantic traffic loading for 6 January 2005. Shanwick OCC

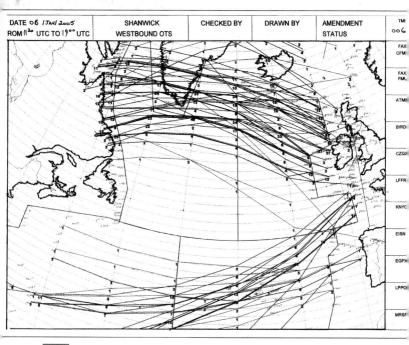

DATE 06 /Jan/ 2005 ROM 1130 UTC TO 1900 UTC	SHANWICK WESTBOUND OTS	CHECKED BY	DRAWN BY	AMENDMENT STATUS	TMI 006

Air 2000 Airbus A320. Author

sets on board. The various co-ordinates of the track are fed into the INS, with the first position being the departure airport. INS is so accurate that each separate parking bay at the airport has its own latitude and longitude, usually displayed on the bay, where it is visible from the flightdeck.

Satellite navigation is increasingly used on the North Atlantic, resulting in very accurate track-keeping.

In fact, this is so precise that aircraft may be one above the other, separated by 1,000ft. To improve safety, an offset method has been introduced, known as Strategic Lateral Offset Procedure (SLOP). This ICAO procedure gives pilots three choices — remain on track; fly one nautical mile right of track; or fly two nautical miles right of track. They must never fly left of track.

Pilots are to use visual means, TCAS or radio communication with other pilots, in deciding which option is safest.

Here is an example of a message for an Oceanic Clearance obtained over the radio:

AC: *'Shanwick, this is Alitalia six five two, estimating DINIM at one one two seven, requesting Track Delta, alternate Track Charlie, flight level three five zero, Mach decimal eight zero, our maximum today will be three six zero.'*

Alitalia 652 is en route from Milan to Toronto, passing over London. The request will have been made approximately 90 minutes before DINIM, which is at 51° north and 15° west, the North Atlantic entry point for Track Delta on this particular day.

All jets flying in North Atlantic airspace use a Mach number percentage of the speed of sound. Mach 80 therefore equals 80% of the speed of sound.

The addition of the 'maximum level' and 'alternate' lets the controller know that, although the current best level requested for the flight is FL350, the aircraft could accept a higher level up to FL360. If the requested route is not available the aircrew would prefer to be off-loaded onto NAT track Charlie, which would be their next most economical route.

The clearance delivery officer (CDO) will input the request into the Flight Data Processing System (FDPS), which displays the flight data to the appropriate planner. A clearance will be formulated and any change annotated to enable the CDO to advise the aircrew when the clearance is issued. This will be radioed to the pilots, who will read back the details, followed by the Track Message Identifier for the particular day.

The CDO will check for the correct readback of both the clearance and the addition of the correct TMI number before returning the flight to the domestic ATC sector.

High-frequency radio coverage of the North Atlantic. Reproduced by kind permission of the OC No 1 AIDU

Radio Transmissions for the North Atlantic

Very High Frequency (VHF) radio used for air traffic control purposes over land depends on 'line of sight' between transmitters and receivers. Effective communication, due to the curvature of the earth, is therefore limited to 200 miles or so. Relay stations throughout the UK and Europe are required to enable the transmissions to reach aircraft in flight. VHF radio is, for this reason, unsuitable for communication where flights cross oceans or sparsely populated continents. Also, because radar operates on the same 'line of sight' principle, it also cannot be applied in these locations.

Much of the traffic in UK airspace is en route between the North Atlantic continent and Europe, crossing the northern area of the Atlantic, where both radar and VHF radio are ineffective. In order to maintain contact with flights over the North Atlantic it is necessary to employ radio bands which are capable of being effective over long distances; for this purpose short wave

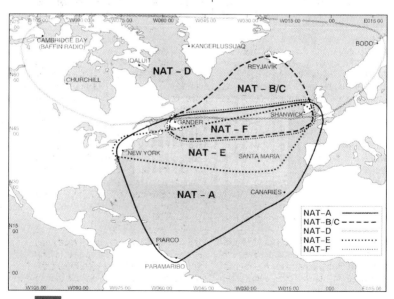

radio is used, although it is now more commonly referred to as High Frequency radio (HF). Also, because of the limitations of radar mentioned earlier, none of the aircraft over the ocean are tracked by controllers. Instead, the control is 'procedural', meaning that separation is achieved by comparing the positions reported by the crews with times and estimated times quoted in flight plans, to ensure that aircraft remain separated by minimum prescribed distances.

One important difference, compared with air traffic control over land, is that the persons who talk to aircrew over the Atlantic on High Frequency radio are not in a position to actually 'control' the flight. Instead, HF messages are handled by radio operators who relay the information to the appropriate oceanic control centre. Where a control action is required — for example a request for a change of flight level — the control centre will pass the approval, or otherwise, to the pilot via the radio operator.

The reception of HF transmissions over long distances can vary from being quite clear and free from interference at one moment to being distorted and completely unreadable the next, and it is for this reason that aircraft are allocated at least two widely separated frequencies, known as 'primary' and 'secondary'. Usually the crew will be able to make contact on the primary frequency, but if this is not possible the secondary frequency will be used.

When a flight crosses from Europe to America, the primary and secondary frequencies for the first part of the crossing will usually be switched at 30° west so that the secondary frequency becomes the primary frequency, and vice versa.

For air traffic purposes, the North Atlantic is divided into five main areas: Shanwick, Santa Maria, Iceland, Gander and New York, known as NARTEL — the North Atlantic Radiotelephony Network. The radio station for traffic in the Shanwick area is at Ballygirreen, near Newmarket-on-Fergus, in County Clare, a few miles north of Shannon airport; it is operated by the Irish Aviation Authority.

During the Atlantic crossing, the aircrew may discontinue maintaining a 'listening watch' on the aircraft radio. Instead, the flight may be contacted from the ground radio station at Ballygirreen by means of a selective calling system, known as Selcal. If the ground station wishes to make contact, a coded radio signal is transmitted to the aircraft. Each aircraft has its own individual code, consisting of two pairs of letters. In each pair the first letter is earlier in the alphabet than the second. For example, BF-AE is acceptable as a Selcal but not FB-EA.

On receipt by the aircraft's decoder a flashing light and/or a chime signal operates on the flightdeck, thereby alerting the crew, who will then reply to the ground station using conventional voice transmissions. Selcal removes the necessity for maintaining a continuous listening watch, which would be particularly onerous on lengthy journeys. Hearing the Selcal code on HF radio identifies the individual aircraft (not the callsign), details of which can be found in specialist publications.

HF Datalink

One possible method of message handling on North Atlantic routes which is under consideration is high-frequency datalink, a less costly means of communication between ground control and aircraft in flight. It will be particularly cost-effective for the North Atlantic as it does not rely on the satellite network. The infrastructure at the Shannon Aeradio Centre at Ballygirreen in Ireland is already in place. Tests are currently being undertaken by Aeronautical Radio Incorporated (ARINC) both for the North Atlantic and worldwide.

Ballygirreen Radio

The radio station at Ballygirreen was established in 1936, making contact with flights in Morse code; this meant that each aircraft had to carry a radio operator to deal with the messages. In 1939 the introduction of teletype enabled the rapid handling of flight details, but the big breakthrough came with the development of radiotelephony in 1948 which effectively did away with the need for the additional crew member.

Westbound Flights

As a transatlantic flight approaches one of the entry points for the London, Shannon or Scottish FIR/UIRs, the pilot will be instructed by the domestic controller to continue with Shanwick on HF. The aircrew will have been given the two appropriate radio frequencies (known as primary and secondary) for their particular flight, and Ballygirreen will be contacted on one of the aircraft's High Frequency radios using the callsign 'Shanwick'. The flight will have received its oceanic clearance from Shanwick sometime earlier, usually on one of the VHF 'clearance delivery' frequencies.

On first contact with the HF operator, the pilot will request a Selcal check to verify that the equipment is functioning correctly. Also, the first 'position report' will be given by the crew and this will be read back by the radio operator. If the crew acknowledge the readback as being correct, the details will be transmitted by direct landline from Ballygirreen to the Shanwick Centre at Prestwick where they are compared with the clearance details for the flight. As the flight progresses across the ocean, position reports are given at the waypoints quoted in the appropriate track message. These will coincide with whole tens of longitude — eg 10° west, 20° west, 30° west, 40° west, etc — and will result in position reports at approximately one-hourly intervals at the most.

As the flight reaches the boundary between two oceanic regions (for example between Shanwick and Gander at 30° west) the message transmitted by the crews in their position reports will be acknowledged by radio operators at both stations; the crews will give their next report to Gander.

The final HF report will be at the waypoint before the boundary of the American or Canadian FIR/UIR, and at this point the HF radio operator will instruct the crew to contact the appropriate domestic control centre on the VHF radio channel.

The majority of flights between Northern Europe and the North American continent will pass through the oceanic

Emirates Airlines Airbus A330. Author

regions of Shanwick and Gander — most European flights to Kennedy Airport at New York do not usually enter the New York Oceanic Region.

Flight Messages

There are eight classifications of reports made by aircrew on HF frequencies:

- POS — Position report at each waypoint across the Atlantic;
- RCL — Request for a clearance;
- RBK — Readback — Confirmation to the Oceanic Area Control Centre of the delivery of an ATC message to a flight, possibly with a reply from the flight;
- RPE — Report of a revised time estimate;
- TAM — Technical Acknowledgement Message;
- SEL — Selcal;
- EMG — An emergency message of Urgency or Distress — eg Mayday;
- MIS — Miscellaneous messages.

Position Reporting Procedures

Reports are given either at designated reporting points or at significant points quoted in the flight plan. Generally, reports are made at approximately one-hourly intervals.

The report is given in latitude and longitude, except that some points may be given names and in such cases these will be quoted. The next position and an estimate of the time at that position is then given, using the next significant point to be crossed by the aircraft. Where the estimate is expected to be incorrect by 3 minutes or more, the fact should be reported to the ATC centre.

Finally, the next position (without an estimate of time over) is given to ATC to enable a close check to be made on the flight at all times. Position reports consist of the following:

- the word 'position';
- the aircraft identity;
- present position;

- time over (in hours and minutes UTC);
- present flight level;
- estimated next position;
- time for estimated position (hours and minutes);
- next significant point;
- further information — eg meteorological or company details.

Flights on routes from east to west (or vice versa) are required to give latitude in degrees and minutes, with longitude only in degrees. (Most North Atlantic tracks have waypoints which occur at whole units of latitude and longitude.)

If the direction of the flight is from south to north, or the opposite, the requirement is for latitude in degrees, with longitude in degrees and minutes.

The following is a typical position report for the North Atlantic:

AC: *'Swissair one one zero, five two north two zero west, one zero two zero, flight level three five zero, estimate five two north three zero west one one zero two, next five one north four zero west.'*

The same message can be written as follows:

'SWISSAIR 110
52 North 20 West 10.20Flight Level 350Estimate 52 North 30 West 11.02Next: 51 North 40 West'

Meteorological information, when required, is transmitted at the end of the message. After the meteorological report the words 'NIL-NIL-NIL' may sometimes be heard. These refer to 'nil icing, nil turbulence, and nil significant weather'.

Message Transfer

The transfer of messages between Ballygirreen and Shanwick is by direct landline, and numerous abbreviations are used to limit the extent of the typescript. All messages commence with the day of the month and the time (for example 161324 indicates the 16th day, time 13.24).

Abbreviations include the following, which are a kind of shorthand used by radio operators at Ballygirreen:

agn	again
apsg	after passing
bndy	boundary
cfms	confirm
sclrnce	clearance
clrsu	clears you
est	estimate
ef	flight level
fm	from
hier	higherl
vl	levell
vg	leaving
mntn	maintain
ms	minus
pos	position
req	request
rl	report leaving
rr	report reaching
rrt	re-route
tfc	traffic
u	you
una	unable

Aircraft callsigns are given with the three-letter airline codes eg BAW176 (Speedbird 176 of British Airways). At the end of the message, the family and the individual frequency is quoted in code — eg TA denotes 'A' family, frequency 5598kHz.

When the report is received from the pilot, the Ballygirreen operator inputs the details into the computer which are then transferred directly to the FDPS computer at Prestwick.

The system automatically checks for errors in the report, bringing them to the attention of the controller for checking and correction. Provided the message is acceptable, the flight data display will be updated. The system will also carry out a conflict probe to ensure that the flight will remain safely separated from other traffic. Only then will a message be sent back to Ballygirreen for onward transmission to the aircraft.

Navigation Problems

The number of cases in which serious navigational errors occur on the North Atlantic are very few. Only a tiny percentage of flights reach the end of the crossing of the Atlantic off course. A pilot can spend his working life flying the routes between Europe and the American continent without ever being off track by more than a few miles.

Nevertheless, mistakes can occur and the advice to flight crews is to be vigilant at all times. As radar is not available, air traffic controllers depend on position reports, which in turn depend on the accuracy of the crew's attention to correct procedure. Many of the mistakes which do happen are extremely simple, and by their nature are difficult to detect. Some of the common errors are quoted here (but remember that serious navigational problems are extremely rare).

■ A one-degree mistake in inserting a waypoint of latitude, especially when the latitude which has been the same for several points is changed by one degree.

■ A request for a route change has been obtained from ATC but the crew forget to re-programme the Inertial Navigation System (INS).

■ The autopilot has been left in the incorrect mode, especially during a period of distraction which has diverted the crew's attention.

■ The clearance given by ATC has been incorrectly heard by the crew; alternatively, the clearance message, although heard correctly, is wrongly interpreted.

Flight crews on the North Atlantic are warned to:

■ Remain alert, especially at the end of a night flight.

■ Take care to follow correct RT procedures.

■ Check carefully on their position before starting the journey.

■ Undertake flightdeck drills carefully.

■ Check thoroughly when loading the initial course into the INS computer.

■ Be aware of simple and absurd situations on the flightdeck which might result in gross errors in navigation.

6. Aeronautical Information

CAUTION — The chart extracts which appear in this publication have been used purely for illustrative purposes. Under no circumstances must the information be relied upon for flight planning, navigation or any other activity related to aviation. Note that the reproductions are not necessarily to the original scale.

Introduction

For the airband radio enthusiast, charts are essential for understanding the significance of the information being heard on the airwaves. They provide detailed information on the various air routes and radio facilities worldwide, and, fortunately, they are all readily available to the general public at very reasonable prices.

Charts showing airspace and airports are obtainable from a large number of suppliers, but they are also available from the producers themselves. There are four main sources in the UK, each providing material covering different aspects of the system.

Separate types of chart are produced for low-level and high-level routes (known as Radio Navigation Charts), civil airports, military airfields and VFR flights.

Although the charts produced by these organisations show basically similar information, there are differences in the colouring systems and in the details of some facilities. Also, there are variations in the areas covered. Obtain a copy of each of the individual catalogues in order that you can compare them and decide which suits you best.

Principal Chart Suppliers

Charts for the UK are available from four main organisations:

- The Royal Air Force
- The European Aeronautical Group
- Jeppesen
- The Civil Aviation Authority

Extract from a high-level en-route RAF chart of UK airspace. Reproduced by kind permission of the OC No 1 AIDU

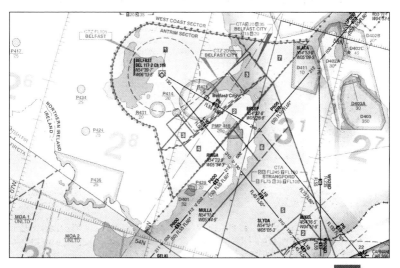

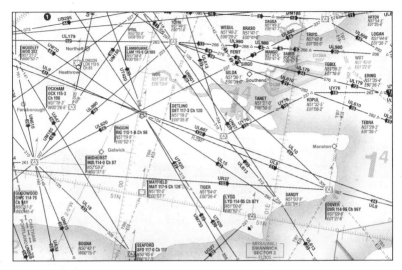

The Royal Air Force

The RAF supplies an excellent range of radio navigation charts for the UK and Europe, produced on good-quality paper. A feature of these charts is that most military routes, North Sea helicopter routes and other military features are also shown.

Two other useful publications are the *Flight Information Handbook* and the *British Isles and North Atlantic En-route Supplement* which provide very detailed information on aviation procedures and airfields for Europe.

In addition to the charts, a variety of other information is available, providing the enthusiast with a mass of invaluable data. Obtain a copy of the RAF's catalogue of Flight Information Publications (called FLIPS), either by post or via its e-mail address. Note that first-time buyers cannot purchase their products via the internet.

The European Aeronautical Group

This company is the main supplier of Aerad charts, which are probably the most well known. Originally owned by British Airways, they are available through many other sales outlets. Its UK charts cover

Extract from a lower airspace RAF chart showing the Belfast terminal area.
Reproduced by kind permission of the OC No 1 AIDU

high and low altitude, including various regions of Europe.

It also provides other worldwide charts, including Standard Instrument Departure Charts, Standard Arrival Charts, Noise Abatement routes for airports, plans of airports, ramp details and details of docking procedures for various aircraft types.

Details of the areas covered can be viewed on its website, through which orders can be placed.

Jeppesen

This company is the largest producer worldwide of charts, flight plans and pilot information.

Many of its radio navigation charts include a comprehensive communications frequency listing on the low-altitude editions. Low-level VFR charts for the

Extract from a High-Level Aerad chart for the UK. European Aeronautical Group Ltd

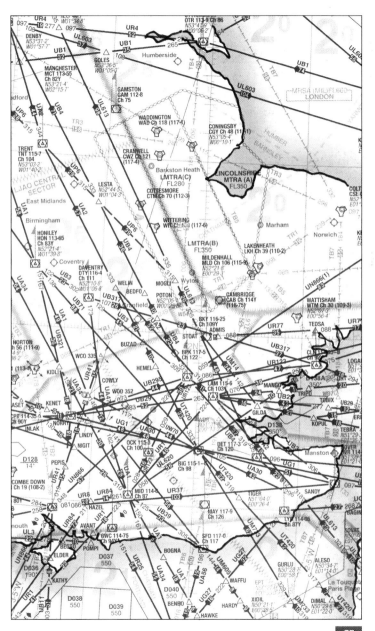

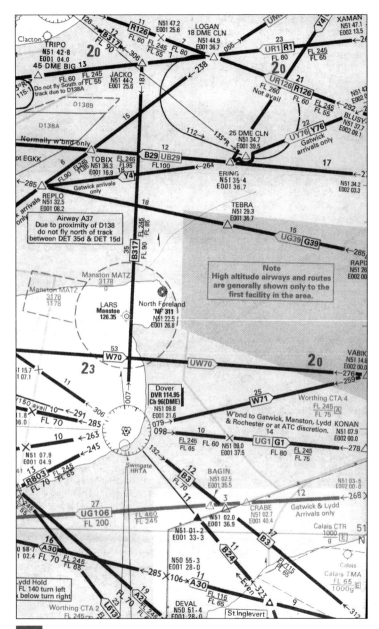

United Kingdom are also available. Its European base is at Frankfurt, Germany, but its products are available via the internet or through one of its UK agents, details of which are included in the appendix.

Many new-generation airliners are provided with electronic Jeppesen data for their flight management systems, and the Jeppesen navigation computers, both mechanical and electronic, are popular with pilots all over the world.

Airplan Flight Equipment (for Civil Aviation Authority publications)

The Civil Aviation Authority distributes a number of charts and other items relating to aeronautical information. They are available from Airplan Flight Equipment, whose address is in Appendix II, or through its website. Note that charts of all UK airfields, including arrival and departure routes, can be printed free of charge directly from the CAA Aeronautical Information Service website.

Also available are charts used principally by pilots flying under Visual Flight Rules. These are based on Ordnance Survey maps and are similar in appearance, showing in full colour roads, motorways, towns and other prominent features but with the addition of airways and other areas of controlled airspace.

Note that the CAA does not produce radio navigation charts.

Understanding the Information

All airways, radio beacons and geographical points are shown on radio navigation charts, although it may take some practice before details can be recognised. The first impression on seeing a chart might probably be of a bewildering mass of lines and figures, but after studying the map the details will start to become clear.

Extract from a Low-Level Aerad chart for the
UK. European Aeronautical Group Ltd

Radio navigation beacons are identified by name and a three-letter abbreviation. 'Dover', for example, is identified as 'DVR' and may be referred to by ATC and by pilots as 'Dover' or 'Delta Victor Romeo'.

Also shown will be the frequency on which the beacon signal is broadcast. In this example 'Dover' transmits on 114.95MHz and by tuning in to this frequency on an airband radio, the signal 'DVR' in Morse code will be heard, provided, of course, that the beacon is within range. All VOR beacons transmit on frequencies between 108MHz and 118Mhz; therefore it is very probable that one can be heard in most areas of the UK.

Compulsory reporting points (often coinciding with VORs) are shown as solid black triangles, located on airways, airways intersections or on boundaries between adjacent control areas. However, in spite of being designated as 'compulsory', not all flights are required to report when passing such points. ATC may sometimes be heard to direct pilots to 'omit position reports on this frequency', and in these cases aircraft may cover large distances without talking to ATC.

Reporting points which are to be used 'on request' are shown as white triangles.

Significant Points

There are hundreds of positions in the UK used to identify navigation points which are not supported by radio facilities on the ground. These locations are used by aircraft with sophisticated navigation capabilities, which are not dependent on radio signals for their accuracy.

Some of the points have a connection with place names in the vicinity, — for example, HALIF (Halifax), NEVIS (Ben Nevis), LESTA (Leicester) etc — but most are simply selected at random. All these positions have five letters, and these are always depicted in capitals. They are known officially as Name Code Designators.

Radio Navigation Beacons

Pilots sometimes refer to positions by names which are not actually those appearing on the charts. 'Glasgow', for example, which is designated Golf Alpha Whiskey, is often quoted as 'the GOW' (rhyming with 'how'). Brookmans Park is called 'The Park', and Pole Hill may be heard as either 'The Pole' or 'The Hill'. Berry Head is known as 'The Head'.

It is easy to plot exactly the location of the VOR beacons shown on the charts by using an Ordnance Survey map. The Landranger 1:50,000 scale is ideal. Each VOR beacon on the charts has the precise latitude and longitude given alongside, and by relating these two figures to the latitude and longitude given on the perimeter of the Ordnance Survey sheet the exact location can be found. As the VOR beacon is situated on the centreline of the airway, the exact position of each airway is also obtained.

Airways and Upper Air Routes

The Air Traffic Service Routes and Upper Air Traffic Service Routes, to give them their official names, are all identified by a letter and a number. On the charts the bearing of the route is given in both directions. Distances between points, in nautical miles, are also shown.

Icelandair Boeing 757. Icelandair

Airways are at least 10 nautical miles wide, with an upper limit of Flight Level 245 and a lower level which is usually around 5,000ft, although some airways can have a base level which might be as high as FL200 (approximately 20,000ft). The base of an airway is usually stepped to facilitate flights descending into terminal areas, or climbing after departure.

Above FL245, in controlled airspace (Class B), airways do not exist. Instead they are replaced with Upper Air Routes, straight-line tracks between reporting points with no specific widths. Since all airspace above FL245 is controlled, flights must comply with ATC instructions. The controller can, subject to military activity, allow aircraft to track away from the upper air routes; these are referred to by ATC and pilots as 'directs'. With modern navigational equipment on board flights, reference to ground-based radio stations is no longer essential so routes away from the beacons are perfectly possible; they are often requested by pilots in order to save time and fuel.

London Terminal Control Centre,
West Drayton, Middlesex. Author

Originally, airways in the UK were referred to by a colour system (Amber, Blue, Green, Red or White) followed by a reference number (for example, Green One, Red Thirty-Seven and so on). This identification method was used when the airways were first established in the 1950s, the colours representing the approximate direction of each route.

On 25 October 1987, to conform with international ICAO standards, the colour system was abandoned and replaced by phonetic references. Amber became Alpha, Blue became Bravo, Green became Golf, Red became Romeo and White became Whiskey.

Some airways' reference numbers were also changed and retitled. Many new letters have now been allocated by ICAO for designating air routes, and these, of course, have no relationship to the old colour system.

A further series of changes took place in November 2003, to comply with the international route designator structure, when several well-known routes were retitled. For example, Golf One/Upper Golf One became Lima 9/Upper Lima 9.

Many of the upper airspace routes do not exist in the airways sytem in lower airspace. The increase in traffic and the need for the most efficient and direct routes have resulted in many new upper air routes being introduced. This has been made possible through the use of sophisticated navigation capabilities of modern aircraft, which no longer rely on the traditional beacons.

An increasing number of aircraft are now routeing on direct tracks using on-board navigational equipment as opposed to ground-based aids, as part of the international strategy for increased capacity and reduced controller workload under a system referred to as Area Navigation.

The distance between VOR beacons is shown alongside the airway in nautical miles. Sometimes the VHF radio frequency for the particular airway is shown, although this cannot be taken as meaning that it will be the only frequency used. Often other alternative frequencies are in operation, and from time to time particular frequencies are changed.

The boundaries between control areas are shown with the information relating to the adjoining areas printed alongside the boundary.

7. Weather and Airfield Data

Introduction

Accurate and up-to-date information about the weather is vital for the safety of a flight. A worldwide system of definitions and codes permits the distribution of weather and airfield data both to airports and to aircraft in flight. This is achieved by several methods — by radio transmissions, by ground communications or by datalink.

Forecasts of weather conditions, as well as the actual weather, for individual airports are obtained through a fairly complex coded process involving hundreds of combinations of weather situations, obtainable by fax, telephone recordings, radio and datalink. These are known as METARs and TAFs.

METARs are the actual weather conditions at individual airfields, and TAFs are forecasts for either a 9-hour period or an 18-hour period. Up-to-the-minute METARs and TAFs can be obtained through the Meteorological Office website at www.metoffice.com/aviation.

At some provincial airports, weather details are available directly from air traffic controllers or Flight Information Service Officers. For airborne flights, information for any airfield may also be requested through the VHF Flight Information Service. For certain principal airports in the UK, and a few on the Continent, conditions are given in pre-recorded broadcasts via VHF and HF Volmet services.

All major airfields have dedicated radio frequencies on which local data is transmitted, sometimes with arrival information and departure information on separate channels. These are referred to as Automatic Terminal Information Services or ATIS.

Volmet Services

The number of flights operating in and out of the principal UK and European airports makes it impractical for controllers to pass weather information directly to every flight. Instead, pre-recorded messages providing airfield conditions in a standardised form are broadcast for many UK, and a few European, airports. The service is known as Volmet, derived from the French word *vol*, meaning flight, and *met*, the abbreviation for weather.

Aircraft in flight are provided with selected airfield conditions through a broadcast system on dedicated radio frequencies under the Volmet system. The United Kingdom has three separate VHF frequencies for the London FIR, while the Scottish and Shannon FIRs each have one VHF frequency. Volmet is also available on HF radio through Shannon Volmet, which covers most European airports, while the Royal Air Force HF Volmet service provides information on many of its operational bases.

Before 1981, all weather broadcasts from major world airports were read over the air by local personnel. Because of individual accents there were sometimes difficulties in clearly understanding these transmissions.

Marconi Space and Defence Systems developed Automatic Volmet to overcome this problem, and since May 1981 it has been in continuous operation around the world. The standard weather report phrases, words and figures were recorded, digitized and stored in a computer memory.

If you are able to listen to Volmet, it may not be obvious that the voice is in fact a composite selection of recordings specially prepared for every possible situation. In many of the original Marconi recordings, the transmission is almost identical to a normal spoken broadcast, with each word having been recorded in a typical sentence and then matched to every other word with which it could be used. For example, the same words spoken during a sentence and at the end of a sentence will sound differently, with stress being applied to a greater or lesser degree. Periods of silence between words and sentences are also provided for. Some of the more recent recordings, however, are not composed to the same high standard as the original Marconi system used in the 1980s.

The weather reports received from the various locations are automatically processed and converted into a code which then selects the appropriate phrases from the memory ready for transmission. Although it is a human voice that is heard, the whole process is fully automatic and operates on a continuous basis. The RAF and Shannon also use this system.

A typical Volmet broadcast, when conditions are good, is as follows:

'This is London Volmet South, this is London Volmet South. London Heathrow at one four five zero. One zero zero degrees nine knots. Cavok. Temperature nine dewpoint four. QNH one zero two five. Nosig.' (Cavok and Nosig are explained later.)

A more complicated transmission, in less favourable conditions, might be:

'Paris Charles de Gaulle at zero seven three zero. Zero eight zero, zero one knots, zero zero five zero metres. Runway visual range zero seven five metres. Fog. Sky obscured. Temperature three, dew point three. QNH one zero two three. Fog dispersal operations are in progress.'

In the UK, Volmet broadcasts cover the following airfields:

London Volmet Main
Amsterdam
Brussels Dublin Gatwick Glasgow
Heathrow Manchester Paris (Charles de Gaulle) Stansted
London Volmet South
Birmingham Bournemouth Bristol Cardiff
Jersey Luton Norwich Southampton
Southend
London Volmet North
Blackpool East Midlands Gatwick Isle of Man Leeds/Bradford Liverpool

Manchester Newcastle Teesside
ScottishVolmet
Aberdeen Belfast Edinburgh Glasgow
Heathrow Inverness Prestwick Stornoway
Sumburgh

The Royal Air Force and Shannon Volmet broadcast details for a large number of airfields on shortwave (HF) frequencies.

Automatic Terminal Information Services (ATIS)

Current conditions at airfields are available via VHF or UHF voice transmissions, sometimes on dedicated frequencies under the ATIS system. Details are amended at regular intervals throughout the day, or whenever there is a significant change. At larger airports arrival information and departure information are sometimes broadcast on separate frequencies.

For individual airfields, many now use digitally recorded information concerning the current conditions broadcast on the appropriate frequency. Each transmission is given an identification letter which is included at the start of the message. When the recording is renewed, the next letter of the alphabet will be used to denote the fact that an amendment has been made.

Each broadcast includes the following information, where relevant:
a) Station name — The name by which the airport is commonly known.
b) Time of observation — The time of the observation in UTC.
c) Surface wind details — The direction of the surface wind and the speed (eg zero seven zero degrees one five knots).
d) Horizontal visibility — Below 5,000 metres the visibility is expressed in metres (eg four zero zero metres). Above 5,000 metres it is given in kilometres.
e) Runway visual range — Runway visual range is given in metres (eg five zero zero metres). Where more than one runway is in use, separate RVR readings may be quoted. RVR is normally quoted for three points along the runway: touchdown, mid-point and stop end.

POLE HILL SIDs   MANCHESTER

GENERAL INFORMATION
1 SIDs reflect Noise Preferential Routeings. See EGCC AD 2.21 for Noise Abatement Procedures.
2 No turns below 757' QNH (500' QFE).
3 Cruising levels at FL270 and below will be allocated en-route by 'Manchester Control', cruising levels above FL270 will be allocated en-route by 'Scottish Control'.
4 Callsign for RTF frequency used when instructed after take-off 'Manchester Control'. On first contact advise callsign/SID designator current altitude and cleared altitude.
5 Maximum IAS 250KT below FL100 unless otherwise authorised.
6 WARNING: RUNWAY 24L/06L. In the event of a missed approach on runway 24R/06R ATC may instruct aircraft which have departed from runway 24L/06L to make a LEFT turn in order to establish separation.

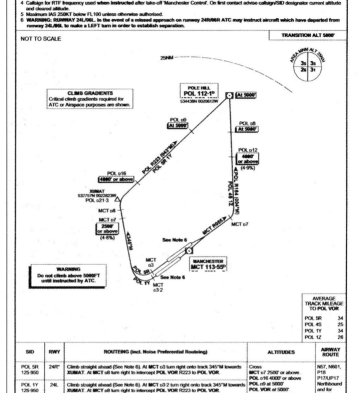

TRANSITION ALT 5000'

SID	RWY	ROUTEING (incl. Noise Preferential Routeing)	ALTITUDES	AIRWAY ROUTE
POL 5R 125·950	24R*	Climb straight ahead (See Note 6). At MCT ᴅ3 turn right onto track 345°M towards XUMAT. At MCT ᴅ8 turn right to intercept POL VOR R223 to POL VOR.	Cross MCT ᴅ7 2500' or above. POL ᴅ16 4000' or above	N57, N601, P18 P17/UP17 Northbound and for aircraft leaving controlled airspace.
POL 1Y 125·950	24L	Climb straight ahead (See Note 6). At MCT ᴅ3·2 turn right onto track 345°M towards XUMAT. At MCT ᴅ8 turn right to intercept POL VOR R223 to POL VOR.	Cross POL ᴅ9 at 5000' POL VOR at 5000'	
POL 4S POL 1Z 125·950	06L† 06R	Straight ahead on MCT VOR R055 (See Note 6). At MCT ᴅ7 turn left to intercept POL VOR R184 to POL VOR.	Cross POL ᴅ12 4000' or above POL ᴅ8 at 5000' POL VOR at 5000'.	

OBSTACLE CLEARANCE
† RWY 06L: Close in obstacles exist below 100' AAL and are not considered for procedure gradients.
* RWY 24R: Close in obstacles exist below 100' AAL and are not considered for procedure gradients.
CHANGE OBSTACLE CLEARANCE.
AERO INFO DATE 25 MAR 04

AMDT 6/04   Civil Aviation Authority

Standard instrument departure routes from Manchester via Pole Hill.
Civil Aviation Authority

f) Weather details — Where appropriate, a description of certain weather conditions is given in plain language (eg rain showers, freezing rain, etc).

g) Cloud details — Where applicable, the extent to which the sky is obscured by cloud is estimated.

■ If the cloud cover is between one eighth and one quarter, the word 'Few' is used to indicate height of the base of the cloud layer in hundreds of feet above aerodrome level.

■ Where the cloud cover is between three-eighths and one half, the word 'Scattered' is used.

■ Where the cloud cover is between five-eighths and seven-eighths the word 'Broken' is used.

■ Where the entire sky is covered by cloud the word 'Overcast' is used.

■ Where no cloud exists the words 'Sky clear' are used.

h) Temperature — Temperature is given in degrees Celsius.

i) Dew point — Dew point is given in degrees Celsius.

j) QNH — QNH is given in millibars.

k) Trend — The trend of the weather conditions may be added if a change is expected soon.

■ If no change is expected, an abbreviation of the words 'No significant change' is given — 'Nosig', pronounced *No-Sig*.

■ Where significant changes are expected the trend of the forecast will be indicated by the words 'Becoming' or 'Tempo'. For example: 'BECOMING from 11.00, 25 to 35 knots, maximum 50 knots, TEMPORARILY from 06.30 until 08.30, 3000 metres. Moderate rain showers'.

'Becoming' is used to indicate that a change is expected to take place at either a regular or irregular rate; 'Tempo' is used to indicate a period of temporary fluctuations to the forecast conditions expected to last less than one hour.

l) Runway state — Runway state given at the touchdown end, mid-point and stop end (eg 'wet, wet, wet').

In conditions where visibility is 10 kilometres or more, the lowest cloud is at a minimum of 5,000ft, there is no cumulonimbus cloud, and there is no precipitation, thunderstorm, shallow fog or low drifting snow, then the relevant parts of the Volmet transmission will be replaced by the expression 'Cavok', derived from 'Cloud And Visibility OK', and pronounced *KAV-O-KAY.*

A typical ATIS transmission would be in the following format:

'*This is Manchester departure information Sierra, at time 07.50, runway for departing aircraft is 24 left, surface wind 160 degrees 10 knots, visibility 20 kilometres, weather nil. Cloud few at 1,400 feet, broken at 3,800 feet, air temperature plus 6, dewpoint plus 2, QNH 1032 millibars. Due work in progress at the end of pier Bravo there will be a displaced centreline on taxiways Juliet and Delta. Be advised there is bird activity reported on runway 24 left. All hold short instructions must be acknowledged and read back. Report aircraft type and departure information Sierra received on first contact with Manchester.*'

8. Current and Future Development

EUROCONTROL Initiatives

Despite the slowing down in the increasing international air traffic levels following the events of 11 September 2001, forecasters still predict that over the next 20 years the number of flights operating in European airspace will grow by 250%.

Being able to handle this traffic efficiently and safely is a challenge which will require some radical developments in the air traffic management process, as well as a great deal of political will. In the complex airspace of Europe, a major hurdle is the fragmentation which exists between national organisations, often using different technology and inconsistent operating procedures.

In the US, for example, each year 20 million flights are managed from 29 control centres. In Europe, 75 control centres, scattered throughout the various states, deal with just 8 million flights. The message is clear enough — co-operation and consistency, and the development of an international management structure, has to be developed.

The first major step towards this goal became reality when the EUROCONTROL concept of the Single European Sky was given legal status on 1 January 2005. This ambitious project seeks to overcome national restrictions and inefficient procedures through the development of more efficient areas of airspace, which are not limited by state boundaries. These will be known as Functional Airspace Blocks (FABs), and already the first moves towards this objective are taking place, although it may take as long as 15 years to be fully developed.

In central Europe, for example, under the Central European Air Traffic Services (CEATS) umbrella, the upper airspace of eight nations will be unified into one control organisation. Austria, Bosnia and Herzegovina, Croatia, the Czech Republic, Hungary, Northern Italy, the Slovak Republic and Slovenia have reached agreement on their airspace coming under the control of the Vienna Air Traffic Control Centre in 2008.

In the UK, the ATC providers in Britain and the Irish Republic are currently investigating the establishment of a single Functional Airspace Block, which would combine their two airspace regions into one.

Experimental work involving TCAS is currently being evaluated by EUROCONTROL. In this diagram Continental Airlines 199 is descending through FL377 to FL350 when TCAS issues a resolution advisory to climb. Speedbird 522, level at FL370, receives a Resolution Advisory to descend. The TCAS warnings are downlinked to the controller's radar screen.

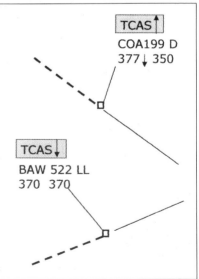

Another EUROCONTROL project, the Flexible Use of Airspace, is aimed at resolving inefficiencies through the restrictions brought about by various states limiting access to their airspace due to military activity. From the end of 2005, regulations will come into effect designed to overcome military and civil airspace restrictions.

The European Air Traffic Management Programme (EATMP) was established as a new approach to meeting European air traffic demand, formerly known as the European Air Traffic Control Harmonisation and Integration Programme, EATCHIP.

This project has been developed as the Air Traffic Management Strategy for 2000+ in collaboration with all interested parties who have a desire to see a fully coherent and efficient airspace structure throughout Europe.

The current programme examines the movement of aircraft from the time at which preparations for a flight take place, perhaps months prior to the actual journey date, through to arrival at the destination airport and to the various procedures that follow on from that point, a concept described as 'gate to gate'.

EUROCONTROL defines the objective of the strategy in the following terms:

'For all phases of flight, to enable the safe, economic, expeditious and orderly flow of traffic through the provision of ATM services which are adaptable and scaleable to the requirements of all users and areas of European airspace. The services shall accommodate demand, be globally inter-operable, operate to uniform principles, be environmentally sustainable and satisfy national security requirements.'

The airlines, many of which have experienced severe financial hardship during the last few years, will need to be reassured that the present level of delays (now at the lowest level ever) will be maintained. They will need to be satisfied that investments in new technology will produce tangible benefits. Improvements in the delays created by inefficiencies in the infrastructure can save airlines huge sums; the same can be said of direct tracks and levels brought about by improved airspace management and more precise navigation capabilities.

The significant changes which are already in place include a reduction in the vertical separation limits (RVSM) between high-level flights from 2,000ft to 1,000ft, a threefold increase in the number of available radio channels for civil traffic, the mandatory use of the Airborne Collision Avoidance System for civil aircraft, and the replanning of airspace sectors and routes in order to improve traffic flows and inter-state co-ordination.

The RVSM programme has already proved its value through improved capacity and delays at a record low.

UK Proposals

In the UK, the Civil Aviation Authority carried out a major comprehensive review of the UK air traffic control strategy in 1996. As a result a two-centre plan was established, involving complementary en-route centres, at Swanwick and at Prestwick, designed to provide backup for each other in the event of a catastrophic failure. Eventually, all en-route traffic will be handled by one of the two centres, including the transfer of current ATC facilities from West Drayton and Manchester.

Although there was a delay of two years at the start of construction of the Scottish centre, building work is now proceeding.

The most ambitious UK project was the construction of a major new £623 million air traffic control centre located at Swanwick, in the south of England, between Portsmouth and Southampton.

The Centre is situated on a 40-acre site with an adjoining nature reserve of 80 acres. Building started in 1991 and handover took place in November 1994. The Centre finally became operational in January 2002. Although there were some initial teething problems, the Centre has proved to be extremely successful.

New systems involving additional computer aid, electronic data exchange and analysis and advanced conflict alert systems allow the current handling capacity to be increased in order to cope with additional traffic over the next 20 years. Two hundred operational controller workstations using 50sq cm 2,000-line vertical colour radar displays are available.

In Shannon, Ireland, a new en-route centre opened in 2004, responsible for 500,000 square kilometres of Irish airspace and 90% of transatlantic traffic.

Airborne Collision Avoidance Systems (ACAS)

The general term for collision avoidance systems operating from aircraft is Airborne Collision Avoidance Systems (ACAS). The only approved ACAS system is use is the Traffic Alert and Collision Avoidance System or TCAS (pronounced Tee-Kass). This is a sophisticated method by which a pilot is alerted to the presence of another aircraft which represents (or may become) a hazard due to its proximity.

As TCAS was a significant factor in the events leading up to the 2002 mid-air collision over southern Germany, the system is described in detail in Chapter 3.

Reduced Separation

One of the most effective ways in which airspace capacity can be enhanced is through the development of reduced separation rules for aircraft, enabling them to operate closer together in every dimension.

Since 1998, vertical separation between high-level traffic has been halved on the North Atlantic from 2,000ft to 1,000ft, and the programme now exists throughout Europe. RVSM is also being implemented in various other parts of the world.

Reduced horizontal separation planning is also in progress for flights on oceanic routes, made possible by improved accuracy of navigation systems and better surveillance methods.

Their work has already resulted in the introduction of parallel route traffic, special routes for flights capable of required area navigation (RNAV), reduced vertical separation minima and lateral and longitudinal separation of 50 nautical miles for some oceanic areas.

Future reductions will be possible as improved surveillance and communication systems become commonplace, ensuring, as always, safety as a first priority.

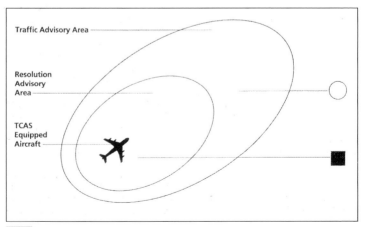

Traffic Advisory Area

Resolution Advisory Area

TCAS Equipped Aircraft

Automatic Dependent Surveillance

North Atlantic trials have been undertaken in oceanic airspace to develop and test the Automatic Dependent Surveillance System (ADS) transmitting routine messages such as position reports and weather conditions between ground stations at Gander, Prestwick and Ballygirreen via the satellite station operated by Arinc at Maryland, USA.

Many modern aircraft are now operating with the latest avionics and flight management computers, known as Future Air Navigation Systems (FANS), which enable them to fly on their preferred direct routes, and the development of ADS will result in this ability being extended to other regions as a matter of routine.

A further development (ADS Broadcast) operates through the aircraft's flight management computer to transmit continuous data concerning the flight's attitude and intentions. This data is received and acted upon by other similarly equipped aircraft in the area and by ground stations, enabling the situational awareness and possible conflict information to be used for increased safety and greater efficiency.

ADS-B information is broadcast twice every second, via the mode S transponder. When the details are presented on the controller's radar screen, the display informs the controller how the information was derived, either by radar or by ADS-B. Trials have shown that ADS-B provides a higher degree of accuracy than traditional radar.

ADS has been in use on North Sea helicopter routes since 1990, transmitting position data to control units via the Inmarsat satellite. One major benefit is the ability to operate perfectly well down to sea level, well below the range of normal radar.

Protected envelope of airspace under the Traffic Alert and Collision Avoidance System. CAA

Datalink and Mode S

The use of datalinking in aviation, compared with the traditional voice system, has been likened to the difference between e-mail and the telephone.

The basic concept is better communication, an essential element of a safe system.

The traditional radio communications will always remain, partly as a backup and partly because some situations may require human intervention, but there is no doubt that sending messages directly to the flightdeck is becoming the norm.

Datalinking has been in regular use at the EUROCONTROL centre at Maastricht since 2003. By 2007, 200 aircraft operating in European airspace are expected to use datalinking routinely, handling around 170,000 messages a year.

Modern flightdeck systems allied to sophisticated VHF and satellite links enable large amounts of data to be transferred between the ground and aircraft in flight. It is no longer necessary for information to be sent by voice over the radio frequencies. Automatic data transfer is much faster and more reliable and can be provided on request from the ground without involving the flight crew.

Mode S (meaning Selective) is an advanced type of transponder capable of being interrogated from the ground for a variety of information. Responses are then transmitted by datalink, independently of the pilots. There are two levels of surveillance available through Mode S: Elementary and Enhanced.

Elementary and Enhanced surveillance was introduced in terminal airspace and on major routes in the UK in March 2005. This permits elementary interrogation by controllers of a selection of 'Downlink Aircraft Parameters', consisting of the squawk, the aircraft altitude to the nearest 25ft, the callsign and the status of the flight. The CAA will issue each aircraft with a 24-bit unique identifier, which means that the interrogation will be received only by

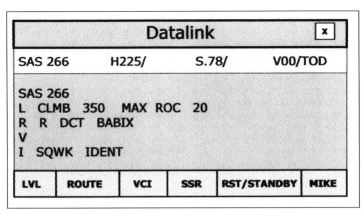

Datalink					☒
SAS 266	H225/		S.78/		V00/TOD

SAS 266
L CLMB 350 MAX ROC 20
R R DCT BABIX
V
I SQWK IDENT

| LVL | ROUTE | VCI | SSR | RST/STANDBY | MIKE |

Datalinking is in regular use at Maastricht Upper Area Control Centre. In this example Scandinavian 266 is instructed to climb to Flight Level 350 with a maximum rate of climb of 2,000ft per minute, to route direct to BABIX, and to squawk ident. The bottom line shows various menus that can be selected by the controller.

that specific aircraft. The enhanced mode enables extra data to be obtained, including ground speed, track angle, turn rate, roll angle, climb rate, magnetic heading, indicated air speed or Mach number and selected flight level.

Elementary surveillance will be introduced in the rest of UK airspace in 2008.

SITA (Société Internationale de Télécommunications Aéronautiques) is an international organisation specialising in worldwide aeronautical communications. Using satellites and VHF ground stations, a vast amount of information is passed between aircraft in-flight and their base stations. More than 75 countries and 500 airlines are involved with SITA. VHF Aircom permits automatic transfer of data from the on-board computers on the flightdeck direct to ground stations. Network terminals on the aircraft give access to a global telecommunications system.

Basic information regarding the aircraft operating systems can be handled as a matter of routine. For example, time of departure, time of landing, engine health monitoring, fuel management, weather conditions and so on can be obtained on request. Oceanic clearances issued by control centres at Reykjavik, Gander, Santa Maria and Prestwick have also been available to North Atlantic flights for some years.

A weather databank for the world's international airports is available and can be accessed directly from the flightdeck, while the aircraft is still on the ground or when it is airborne. Queries initiated by the pilot are responded to within seconds.

CNS/ATM

This is the concept of Communication, Navigation, Surveillance and Air Traffic Management which was originally known by the term Future Air Navigation Systems (FANS).

These incorporate advanced avionics packages which enable the transfer of accurate information and data messages between the ground and the aircraft, helping to shift the emphasis away from traditional control and more towards management of the airspace where pilots play an active role in deciding an aircraft's flight profile.

Highly accurate and reliable position reporting allows more flexibility in following desired tracks and levels. The position of an aircraft can be planned in four dimensions, where the crossing of a particular waypoint can be arranged within a specified time frame, well ahead of any possible conflict that might arise.

These systems rely on the use of Mode S transponders which have the benefit of a unique 'for life' label for every aircraft, meaning that messages can be addressed directly to specific flights while ignoring all others.

Ongoing trials of an appropriate method of achieving this objective were completed under the umbrella of the EOLIA project (European pre-Operational Datalink Applications) organised by a European consortium of industry leaders. These are NATS, Aérospatiale-Matra, Dutch NLR, Sofreavia, Airsys ATM, Airbus, Air France and British Airways.

Four kinds of operational processes were evaluated and studied in live flight trials during which datalink messages and instructions were exchanged between ground control and the flightdeck. The benefits will be an increase in the reliability of messages, standardised message formats, reduced RT overloading, easier monitoring of flights, the selective message ability and improved security of messages.

Galileo and EGNOS Positioning Systems

These two projects involve the provision of satellite networks across Europe to improve navigation for aircraft and other forms of transport.

The European Geostationary Navigation Overlay System (EGNOS) became operational in 2003, providing a navigation service extending from Iceland to Africa, improving the normal accuracy of the Global Positioning System from 20 metres to 5 metres.

EGNOS will eventually be replaced by the European satellite navigation system, Galileo, which is intended for use by all forms of transport and will consist of up to 50 medium earth satellites, planned for introduction in 2008. It is being funded jointly by the European Space Agency (ESA) and the European Commission, and a consortium of industry leading companies.

Close-up of one of the turbofans on the Airbus A330. Qatar Airways

Free Flight

Free flight is an American concept, put forward by the Federal Aviation Administration. The proposal involves the transfer of responsibility for determining flight paths to the pilot of an aircraft while air traffic control acts as a system manager monitoring the relevant position of every flight in the system and intervening where necessary to resolve possible conflicts. New technology will make the idea practical through the use of CNS (Communications, Navigation and Surveillance). Although there are no clear definitions, there is little doubt in the aviation industry that major changes will be necessary to deal with future traffic levels.

In America a trial of the system, referred to as Flight 2000, started at the end of 1999 between Hawaii and Alaska using satellite-based navigation datalink conflict alert and safety alert. Air space users flight-plan every flight in four dimensions: laterally, longitudinally, vertically and in time. Computers predict conflicts and modify the flight plans to avoid bottlenecks and possible conflicts. The position and intentions of every aircraft will be known to all others in the vicinity. Each aircraft will occupy a protected zone of airspace which can never be allowed to overlap with another. Beyond the protected zone is an alert zone, which provides early warning of possible problems.

Major savings to airlines are anticipated. American Airlines, for example, reckons that a reduction in flight time of only two minutes for every flight will result in a saving of $40 million per year.

The EUROCONTROL definition of free flight is as follows:

'Free Flight involves airspace without fixed route structures in which suitably equipped aircraft will be able to fly user-preferred four dimensional routes and may take responsibility for their own separation. The eventual situation will be that all aircraft will be able to fly under Free Flight mode. Access to this airspace by less capable aircraft will be subject to acceptance by the Air Traffic Management Services whereby access by capable aircraft is implicit. Free Flight mode is defined as operations comprising both free routeing and autonomous separation.'

Summary

In summary, many new initiatives are planned for future air traffic management improvements, both in Europe and in other parts of the world. All are based on the concept of better technology to assist controllers, together with improved airspace capacity.

Over the next 10 to 15 years there will be a shift towards more automated support systems, the automation of routine tasks, improved situational awareness for pilots and controllers, and a transfer of tasks from the controllers to the pilots.

JMC Airlines Airbus A330. Author

Appendices

Abbreviations

The following lists cover a selection of abbreviations of the most common situations, but they are not exhaustive.

Many abbreviations and acronyms are used in aviation terminology. Those annotated with an asterisk are normally spoken as complete words. The remainder are normally spoken using the constituent letters rather than the spelling alphabet.

AARA	Air to Air Refuelling Area
ACARS	Airborne communication, addressing and reporting system
ACAS	Airborne collision avoidance system
ACC	Area control centre or area control
ADF	Automatic direction-finding equipment
ADR	Advisory route
ADS	Automatic dependent surveillance system
ADT	Approved Departure Time
AFIS	Aerodrome flight information service
AFS	Aeronautical Fixed Service
AGL	Aeronautical Fixed Telecommunications Network
AGAS	Action Group for ATM Safety
AFTN	Above ground level
AIAA	Area of Intense Air Activity
AIC	Aeronautical information circular
AIP	Aeronautical information publication
AIRAC*	Aeronautical information regulation and control
AIRPROX*	Aircraft Proximity
AIS	Aeronautical information services
AMA	Approach Monitoring Aid
AMS	Aeronautical Mobile Service
AMSL	Above mean sea level
APALS	Autonomous Precision Approach and Landing System
APHAZ	Aircraft Proximity Hazard
ARINC	Aeronautical Radio Incorporated
ASMI	Aerodrome Surface Movement Indicator
ASR	Altimeter Setting Region
ATA	Actual time of arrival
ATA	Aerial Tactics Area
ATC	Air traffic control (in general)
ATCC	Air traffic control centre
ATCRU	Air traffic control radar unit
ATD	Actual time of departure
ATFM	Air Traffic Flow Management
ATIS*	Automatic terminal information service
ATM	Air Traffic Management
ATS	Air traffic services
ATSU	Air Traffic Service Unit
ATZ	Aerodrome traffic zone
BRNAV	Basic Area Navigation
CAA	Civil Aviation Authority
CAC	Centralised approach control
CANP	Civil Aviation Notification Procedure
CAS	Controlled airspace
CEATS	Central European Air Traffic Services
CFMU	Central Flow Management Unit
CTA	Control Area
CTOT	Calculated Take-off Time
CTR	Control Zone
D...	Danger area (followed by identification)
DCL	Departure Clearance
DEP*	Departure message
DF	Direction finding
DFR	Departure Flow Regulation
DFTI	Distance from touchdown indicator
DGNSS	Differential Global Navigation Satellite System
DGPS	Differential Global Positioning System

DME	Distance measuring equipment		HCS	Host Computer System
DVOR	Doppler VOR		HF	High frequency
			HIRO	High Intensity Runway Operations
EAT	Expected approach time		HJ	Sunrise to sunset
EATCHIP	European ATC Harmonisation and Integration Programme		HMR	Helicopter Main Route
			HN	Sunset to sunrise
EATMP	European Air Traffic Management Programme		H+	Hours plus minutes past the hour
ECAC	European civil aviation conference		HX	No specific working hours
EET	Estimated elapsed time		IATA	International Air Transport Association
EGNOS	European Geostationary Navigation Overlay System		ICAO	International Civil Aviation Organisation
EOBT	Estimated Off-Blocks Time		ICF	Initial contact frequency
ETA	Estimated time of arrival		IDENT*	Identification
ETD	Estimated time of departure		IFR	Instrument Flight Rules
ETOT	Estimated Take-off Time		ILS	Instrument landing system
			IMC	Instrument meteorological conditions
FAB	Functional Airspace Blocks			
FANS	Future air navigation systems		INFO*	Information
FAST	Final Approach Spacing Tool		INS	Inertial navigation system
FDPS	Flight Data Processing System		IRVR	Instrumented Runway Visual Range
FEATS	Future European ATS systems concept		Kg	Kilograms
FIC	Flight information centre		kHz	Kilohertz
FIR	Flight information region		Km	Kilometres
FIS	Flight information service		Kn	Knots
FISO	Flight Information Service Officer		LARS	Lower airspace radar service
FL	Flight level		LACC	London Area Control Centre (Swanwick)
FLIP	Flight information publication			
FMS	Flight management system		LJAO	London Joint Area Organisation
FMP	Flow Management Position			
FPS	Flight Progress Strip		LORAN*	Long-range air navigation system
FPPS	Flight plan processing system			
GAT	General Air Traffic		LSB	Lower side band
GCA	Ground controlled approach		LTCC	London Terminal Control Centre (West Drayton)
GLONASS	Global Orbiting navigation satellite system (Russia)			
			MACC	Manchester Area Control Centre
GMC	Ground movement control			
GMR	Ground movement radar		MAS	Middle airspace service
GMT	Greenwich Mean Time		MASPS	Minimum Aircraft System Performance Specification
GNSS	Global navigation satellite system			
			MATO	Military air traffic operations
GPS	Global positioning system (USA)		MATZ*	Military Aerodrome Traffic Zone
H24	Continuous day and night service		MB	Millibars
			MDA	Minimum Descent Altitude

MEDA	Military Emergency Division Aerodrome	POB	Persons on Board
MET*	Meteorology	PPI	Plan position indicator
METAR	Aerodrome actual weather	PPR	Prior permission required
MF	Medium Frequency	PRNAV	Precision Area Navigation
MHz	Megahertz		
MIL	Military	QDM	Magnetic bearing to facility
MLS	Microwave landing system	QDR	Magnetic bearing from facility
MMR	Multi-Mode Receiver	QFE	Height above airport elevation
MNPS	Minimum navigation performance specification		or runway threshold
MRSA	Mandatory radar service area	QFF	Atmospheric pressure converted to mean sea level
MSS	Message Storage and Switching System	QGH	Controlled descent through cloud
MTA	Military training area	QNE	Indicated height on landing with altimeter subscale set at 1013.25 millibars
NAS	National Airspace System		
NARTEL	North Atlantic Radio Telephony Network	QNH	Altitude above sea level based on local station atmospheric pressure
NATS	National Air Traffic Services		
NDB	Non-directional radio beacon	QTE	True bearing
NERC	New En-route Centre (see LACC)	RAF	Royal Air Force
		RAS	Radar Advisory Service
NOTA	Northern Oceanic Transition Area	RC	Radar corridor
		RCC	Rescue Co-ordination Centre
NOTAM*	Notices of aeronautical information	RHSM	Reduced Horizontal Separation Minima
NSC	New Scottish Centre	RIS	Radar Information Service
		RNAV	Area navigation
OAC	Oceanic area control	ROT	Runway Occupancy Times
OACC	Oceanic area control centre	RPS	Regional pressure setting
OAT	Operational air traffic	RTF	Radiotelephony
OCA	Obstacle clearance altitude	RVC	Radar Video Corridor
OCH	Obstacle clearance height	RVR	Runway Visual Range
OCL	Obstacle clearance limit	RVSM	Reduced Vertical Separation Minima
ODID	Operational Display and Input Development		
OM	Outer Marker	SAM	Slot Allocation Message
ORCA	Oceanic Route Clearance Authorisation	SAR	Search and Rescue
		SCATCC	Scottish Air Traffic Control Centre
PANS	Procedures for Air Navigation Services	SELCAL*	A system which permits the selective calling of individual aircraft over radiotelephone channels
PAPI*	Precision Approach Path Indicator		
PAX	Passengers	SES	Single European Sky
PDC	Pre-departure Clearance	SID*	Standard Instrument Departure
PDCS	Pre-departure Clearance System	SIGMET*	Significant meteorological information which may affect aircraft safety
PHARE	Programme for Harmonised Research in EUROCONTROL		

SITA	Société Internationale de Télécommunications Aéronautiques
SLOP	Strategic Lateral Offset Procedure
SMI	Standard Message Identifier
SNOWTAM*	Special series NOTAM concerning snow, ice or slush at airfields
SOTA	Shannon Oceanic Transition Area
SPECIAL*	Special meteorological report
SR	Sunrise
SRG	Safety Regulation Group
SS	Sunset
SSB	Single Side Band Radio
SSR	Secondary surveillance radar
SST	Supersonic transport
STAR*	Standard Arrival Route
STCA	Short Term Conflict Alert
STOL	Short Take-off and Landing
SWORD	System for worldwide operational route data
TACAN*	Tactical Area Navigation Aid
TAF*	Terminal Aerodrome Forecast
TCAS	Traffic alert and collision avoidance system
TMA	Terminal control area
TMI	Track Message Identification
TVOR	Terminal VOR
UAR	Upper air route
UAS	Upper air space
UHF	Ultra High Frequency
UIR	Upper flight information region
USB	Upper Side Band
UTA	Upper control area
UTC	Co-ordinated universal time
VASI	Visual approach slope indicator
VDF	Very high frequency direction-finding
VFR	Visual Flight Rules
VHF	Very high frequency
VIP	Very important person
VMC	Visual meteorological conditions
VOLMET*	Meteorological information for aircraft in flight
VOR	VHF omnidirectional range (beacon)
VORTAC	Combined VOR and TACAN
VRP	Visual Reference Point
WIP	Work in progress
ZULU*	UTC Time

Glossary of Terms

The following definitions are commonly used in Air Traffic Management and Control:

Advisory Area:
A designated area where air traffic advisory service is available.

Advisory Route:
A designated route along which air traffic advisory service is available.

Aerodrome Control Service:
Air traffic control service for aerodrome traffic.

Aerodrome Traffic:
All traffic on the manoeuvring area of an aerodrome and all aircraft operating in the vicinity of an aerodrome.

Aerodrome Traffic Zone:
Airspace of defined dimensions established around an aerodrome for the protection of aerodrome traffic.

Aeronautical Mobile Service:
All radio communication service between aircraft stations and aeronautical stations, or between aircraft stations.

Aeronautical Station:
A land station in the aeronautical mobile service. In certain instances, an aeronautical station may be placed on board a ship or an earth satellite.

Aircraft Station:
A mobile station in the aeronautical mobile service on board an aircraft.

Air/Ground Communications:
Two-way communication between aircraft and stations or locations on the surface of the earth.

Air Traffic:
All aircraft in flight or operating on the manoeuvring area of an aerodrome.

Air Traffic Control Centre:
A term used in the United Kingdom to describe a unit providing en-route air traffic control services.

Air Traffic Control Clearance:
Authorisation for an aircraft to proceed under conditions specified by an air traffic control unit.

Air Traffic Services:
A generic term meaning variously, flight information service, alerting service, air traffic advisory service, air traffic control service, area control service, approach control service or aerodrome control service.

Airway:
A control area or part of a control area established in the form of a corridor equipped with radio navigation aids.

Altitude:
The vertical distance of a level, a point or an object considered as a point, measured from mean sea level.

Approach Control Service:
A service provided by ATC for arriving, departing and overflying traffic.

Approved Departure Time:
An allocated take-off time calculated from the elapsed flight time between the aerodrome of departure and the point at which the regulated flow is effective.

Area Control Service:
A unit established to provide air traffic control service to controlled flights in control areas under its jurisdiction.

Area Navigation (RNAV):
Navigational method permitting aircraft to operate on any desired flight path within coverage of ground-based navigational aids or self-contained navigational aids or a combination of both.

Automatic Dependent Surveillance (ADS):
A surveillance technique in which aircraft automatically provide, via a datalink, data derived from on-board navigation and position-fixing systems, including aircraft identification four-dimensional position and additional data as appropriate.

Automatic Terminal Information Service:
The provision of current, routine information to arriving and departing aircraft by means of continuous and repetitive broadcasts throughout the day or a specified portion of the day.

Blind Transmission:
A transmission from one station to another station in circumstances where two-way communication cannot be established but where it is believed that the called station is able to receive the transmission.

Broadcast:
A transmission of information relating to air navigation that is not addressed to a specific station or stations.

Clearance Limit:
The point to which an aircraft is granted an air traffic control clearance.

Control Area:
Controlled airspace extending upwards from a specified limit above the surface of the earth, to a specified upper limit.

Controlled Airspace:
An airspace of defined dimensions within which air traffic control service is provided to IFR flights and to VFR flights in accordance with the airspace classification.

Control Zone:
A controlled airspace extending upwards from the surface of the earth to a specified upper limit.

Controller/Pilot Data Link Communications:
A means of communication between controllers and pilots using datalink for ATC communications.

Co-ordinated Universal Time (UTC):
A combination of international Atomic and Universal Time, which has replaced Greenwich Mean Time as the accepted international standard. It is always within 0.5 seconds of Universal Time.

Cruising level:
A level maintained during a significant portion of a flight.

Decision Height:
A specified height in a precision approach at which a missed approach must be initiated if the required visual reference to continue the approach has not been established.

Expected Approach Time:
The time at which ATC expects that an arriving aircraft, following a delay, will leave the holding point to complete its approach for a landing.

Flight Level:
A surface of constant atmospheric pressure, which is related to a specific pressure datum, 1013.25mb, and is separated from other such surfaces by specific pressure intervals.

Flight Plan:
Specified information provided to air traffic services units, relative to an intended flight or portion of a flight of an aircraft.

Flight Visibility:
The visibility forward from the flightdeck of an aircraft.

General Air Traffic:
Flights operating in accordance with civil air traffic procedures.

Heading:
The direction in which the longitudinal axis of an aircraft is pointed, usually expressed in degrees from North (true, magnetic, compass or grid).

Heavy:
Aircraft officially classified as 'heavy'.

Height:
The vertical distance of a level, a point, or an object considered as a point measured from a specified datum.

IFR Flight:
A flight conducted in accordance with the Instrument Flight Rules.

Instrument Meteorological Conditions:
Meteorological conditions expressed in terms of visibility, horizontal and vertical distance from cloud less than the minima specified for visual meteorological conditions.

Level:
A generic term relating to the vertical position of an aircraft in flight and meaning variously, height, altitude or flight level.

Middle Airspace Service:
A radar service provided by an Air Traffic Control Area Radar Unit in the airspace between FL100 and FL245.

Minimum Sector Altitude:
The lowest altitude which may be used under emergency conditions which will provide a minimum clearance of 1,000ft above all obstacles located in an area contained within a sector of a circle of 25 nautical miles radius centred on a radio aid to navigation.

Missed Approach Procedure:
The procedure to be followed if, after an approach, a landing is not effected.

Operational Air Traffic:
Flights operating in accordance with military air traffic service procedures.

Quadrantal Cruising Level:
Specified cruising levels determined in relation to magnetic track within quadrants of the compass.

Radar Control:
The term used to indicate that radar-derived information is employed directly in the provision of an air traffic control service.

Radar Vectoring:
Provision of navigational guidance to aircraft in the form of specific headings, based on the use of radar.

Reporting Point:
A specified geographical location at which the position of an aircraft is reported.

Runway Visual Range:
The range over which the pilot of an aircraft on the centreline of a runway can see the runway surface markings or the lights delineating the runway or identifying its centreline.

Secondary Surveillance Radar:
A system of radar using ground interrogators and airborne transponders to determine the position of an aircraft.

Significant Points:
Geographical positions for air navigation, defined by latitude and longitude, with names consisting of five letters.

Special VFR Flight:
A VFR flight cleared by ATC to operate within a control zone under meteorological conditions below VMC (ICAO definition). Note that in the UK the position differs in that special VFR flight is permitted in a control zone which is Class A airspace or in any other control zone in instrument meteorological conditions or at night, provided the aircraft remains clear of cloud and in sight of the surface.

Track:
The direction of the path of an aircraft over the ground usually expressed in degrees from North.

Transition Altitude:
The altitude at or below which the vertical position of an aircraft is controlled by reference to altitudes.

Transition Layer:
The airspace between the transition altitude and the transition level. The depth of this layer will normally be insignificant and will never exceed 500ft.

Transition Level:
The lowest flight level above the transition altitude. It will vary in accordance with the relationship between the QNH and the standard pressure datum.

VFR Flight:
A flight conducted in accordance with the Visual Flight Rules.

Visual Meteorological Conditions:
Meteorological conditions expressed in terms of visibility, distance from cloud, and ceiling, equal to or better than specified minima.

Standard Phrases

Certain words and phrases are used in air traffic control, and they have the meanings given below. However, those with an asterisk are not recognised as standard words or phrases.

Acknowledge — Let me know that you have received and understood this message.

Affirm — Yes.

Approved — Permission for proposed action granted.

Break — Indicates the separation between messages.

Break Break — Indicates separation between messages when very busy.

Build-up* — Storm clouds.

Cancel — Annul the previously transmitted clearance.

Centrefix — Instrument navigation to a runway centreline without reference to ground facilities.

Charlie* — Correct.

Charlie Bravo* — Cumulonimbus storm clouds.

Check — Examine a system or procedure (no answer is normally expected).

Cleared — Authorised to proceed under the conditions specified.

Climb — Authorisation to climb to a higher (specified) level.

Confirm — Have I correctly received the following . . ? or Did you correctly receive this message?

Contact — Establish radio contact with . . .

Continue (a heading) — Remain on the present heading until advised.

Correct — That is correct.

Correction — An error has been made in this transmission (or message indicated). The correct version is . . .

Descend — Authorisation to descend to a lower (specified) level.

Disregard — Consider that transmission as not sent.

Expedite — Increase rate of climb or descent to a higher than normal rate.

Freecall — Change to a frequency where a transfer has not been co-ordinated.

Fox Echo* — QFE.

How do you read — What is the readability of my transmission?

I say again — I repeat for clarity or emphasis.

Leave (or leaving) — Point at which an aircraft has left a particular level, either climbing or descending.

Maintain (a level) — Remain at the present level until advised.

Monitor — Listen out on (frequency).

Negative — No, or Permission not granted, or That is not correct.

Over — My transmission is ended and I expect a response from you.

Out — This exchange of transmissions is ended and no response is expected (the words 'over and out' are not normally used).

Out of* — Leaving a particular level (the correct word to use is Leaving).

Pass your Message — Proceed with your message.

Pilot's Discretion — The commencement of a climb or descent is at the discretion of the pilot.

Read back — Repeat all, or the specified part, of this message back to me exactly as received.

Reaching — Point at which an aircraft has achieved a particular level.

Repeat* — Repeat some or all of a message (the correct phrase is Say Again).

Report — Pass requested information.

Request — I should like to know . . . or I wish to obtain . . .

Roger — I have received all your last transmission. Note: Under no circumstances to be used in reply to a question requiring a direct answer in the affirmative (Affirm) or negative (Negative).

Say Again — Repeat all, or the following part of your last transmission.

Self Position* — Instrument navigation to a runway centreline without reference to ground facilities (see Centrefix).

Speak Slower — Reduce your rate of speech.

Standby — Wait and I will call you. Note: No onward clearance to be assumed.

Switch* — Change frequency.

Uniform Frequency* — UHF frequency.

Vacating* — Point at which a climb or descent is commenced (correct word is 'leaving').

Verify — Check and confirm.

Victor Frequency* — VHF frequency.

Victor Mike* — Visual Meteorological conditions.

Vortex* — Turbulent wake left by a heavy category aircraft.

Wilco — I understand your message and will comply with it (abbreviation for 'will comply').

Words Twice — Communication is difficult. Please say all words twice.

Useful Addresses

Air Traffic Control Centres

London Area Control Centre
Sopwith Way, Swanwick
Southampton, Hampshire SO31 7AY
Tel: 01489 584875

London Terminal Control Centre
Porters Way, West Drayton
Middlesex UB7 9AX
Tel: 01895 445566

Scottish and Oceanic Air Traffic Control Centre
Atlantic House, Sherwood Road
Prestwick, Ayrshire KA9 2NR
Tel: 01292 479800

Manchester Area Control Centre
Manchester Airport
Wythenshawe
Manchester M90 2PL
Tel: 0161 499 5300

Other Organisations

National Air Traffic Services Ltd
Brettenham House South
Lancaster Place
London WC2E 7EN
Tel: 020 7309 8666
Web: www.nats.co.uk

Civil Aviation Authority
CAA House
45-59 Kingsway
London WC2B 6TE
Tel: 020 7379 7311
Web: www.caa.co.uk

Aeronautical Information Service
Control Tower Building
London Heathrow Airport
Hounslow
Middlesex TW6 1JJ
Tel: 020 8745 3456
Web: www.ais.org.uk

Irish Aviation Authority
Aviation House, Hawkins Street
Dublin 2
Ireland
Tel: 353 1 6031100
Web: www.iaa.ie

International Civil Aviation Organisation
1000 Sherbrooke Street West
Suite 400
Montreal
Quebec
Canada H3A 2R2
Tel: (514) 285 8222
Web: www.icao.int

EUROCONTROL
European Organisation for the Safety of Air Navigation
Rue de la Fusée 96
B-1130 Brussels
Tel: 32.2.729 90 11
Web: www.eurocontrol.int

College of Air Traffic Control
National Air Traffic Services
Bournemouth (Hurn) Airport
Christchurch
Dorset BH23 6DF
Tel: 01202 472334

Charts and Publications Suppliers
Airplan Flight Equipment
1A Ringway Trading Estate
Shadowmoss Road
Manchester M22 5LH
Tel: 0161 499 0023
Fax: 0161 499 0298
Web: www.afeonline.com

Westward Documedia Ltd
37 Windsor Street
Cheltenham
Glos GL52 2DG
Tel: 01242 235151
Fax: 01242 584139
Web: www.documedia.co.uk

European Aeronautical Group UK Ltd
Hersham House
Lyon Road
Walton-on-Thames KT12 3PU
Tel: 01932 704200
Fax: 01932 267572
Web: www.euronautical.com

Royal Air Force
Flight Information Publications
No. 1 AIDU
RAF Northolt
West End Road, Ruislip
Middlesex HA4 6NG.
Tel: 020 8845 2300
Fax: 020 8841 1078
Web: www.aidu.mod.uk

Transair Pilot Shop
Shoreham Airport
Shoreham by Sea
West Sussex
BN43 5PA
Tel: 01273 466000
Web: www.transair.co.uk